Strength to Stand
Equipping the Church for Impact through
Apostolic-Prophetic Leadership

Naomi Dowdy

NAOMI DOWDY MINISTRIES
DALLAS, TX

Strength to Stand
Equipping the Church for Impact through Apostolic-Prophetic Leadership

Naomi Dowdy

*Strength to Stand: Equipping the Church for Impact through
Apostolic-Prophetic Leadership*

Author's Note: As part of my overall effort to begin restoring proper honor, respect, and dignity to the five-fold offices of the Church, I have chosen to capitalize Apostle, Prophet, Pastor, Teacher, and Evangelist throughout this book. Though some may question this decision, I have made it in order to help emphasize the importance of these offices. I trust you will not stumble over the capitalization, but will join with me in many different efforts to contribute toward the worthy goal of seeing respect restored to these ministry offices, God's gifts to the body of Christ.

ISBN: 978-1-934201-05-3

Printed in Singapore
5 4 3 2 1 07 08 09 10 11

Contents

Introduction

THE RESTORATION OF APOSTLES and Prophets in the Church today has been underway for quite some time, and much has been said and written about these offices and those who minister from them. Anyone interested in apostolic-prophetic ministry can find a number of books that address and explain different functions and characteristics of Apostles and Prophets, and different approaches to apostolic-prophetic ministry. I thank God for all the revelation that has come to us over the past several years, and I honor those who have served and are still serving the body of Christ as Apostles and Prophets.

Why then, do we need another book dealing with the topic of Apostles and Prophets? Frankly, I believe we need additional information and revelation on this subject because there are many people across the religious and denominational spectrum who still do not understand God's plan and purpose for this new season of the Church in which we are currently living.

Statistics show there are more churches in the world today than ever before in history; there are also more Christians in the world today than ever before. At the same time, most of us would agree that our daily headlines indicate an alarming decline in moral values and respect for human life. These facts being true, we must ask ourselves what is missing. What should be happening in and through our churches, and in and through the life of every believer, that is not happening? Why are we failing to impact our societies as we should? Why are some people disillusioned with the Church or its leaders, and even with their own personal walk with God?

Jesus made a strong declaration in Matthew 16:18: "...I will build my Church, and the gates of hell will not overcome it." Instead of efforts to build the Church of Jesus Christ today, we see efforts to fragment the Church even more than it already is. We see many Church leaders allowing worldly values to encroach, rather than addressing the missing ingredients and getting the Church back in sync with God's Word.

In view of these realities, we must ask ourselves a few questions:

- How can we develop in the Church the kind of believers who can establish and represent God's Kingdom as He desires?
- How do we fulfill the Great Commission, but also experience the fullness of Christ's purpose, as expressed in Ephesians 4:11, 12?
- How did we get so far off track?
- What kind of leaders does the Church need to get us back on track?

I will address these critical questions and more throughout this book. I will also suggest some proven ways to first *understand* God's plan and then to *accomplish* God's plan.

I will also provide some examples and models as practical ways through which we can see God "reverse the curse" once again and see the Church arise to become the victorious Church He intends for us to be.

Section I:

A New Paradigm for Leadership

CHAPTER 1

God Is On the Move

YOU AND I ARE LIVING in the most dynamic hour the Church has ever known. We are seeing mega-churches growing in the most unlikely countries, cities, and neighborhoods, and we are seeing cross-cultural Pastors leading these churches. The nations that are becoming the greatest missions-sending nations are no longer located in the western hemisphere. Western countries are no longer the primary exporters of Christianity, but have been replaced by nations such as South Korea, Nigeria, and others. These pioneers, Pastors, or missionaries (as we would have called them in the past), are stirring the Church world. In many places across the world, miracles are so expected today that being in church is like reading the Book of Acts.

Along with this dynamic growth and the miracles we are seeing, we are also experiencing the restoration of God's gifts—His five-fold ministry gifts recorded in Ephesians 4:11—to the Church. For generations God has been bringing progressive revelation to the hearts of those who have an "ear to hear what the Spirit is saying to the Church." These "hearers" became known as Prophets. They began not only hearing what the Spirit was saying, they also began announcing God's new season.

If we look back at what has been happening over these last few decades, we must admit that God in His sovereignty has been moving to prepare His Church for its great purpose and destiny. Many leaders have been praying and fasting for God's Kingdom to come and His will to be done. God is answering that prayer. However, for some the reality of God's Kingdom has been difficult to receive because of training, traditions, and the affects of the Dark Ages, which still hold the Church captive even today.

Some writers, especially Dr. C. Peter Wagner, have identified the impact of the restoration (recognition, acceptance) of now all five of these offices instead of only the usual three offices of Pastor, Evangelist, and Teacher. This growing acknowledgement and acceptance of these offices has caused new descriptive language to be birthed. Specifically, Wagner is using such descriptive terms as "Post-Denominationalism," "The New Apostolic Reformation," and his most recent, "The Second Apostolic Age." Wagner's writings and terminology have been welcomed by many, but have also been met with strong opposition concerning the offices of Apostle and Prophet in today's Church. This opposition has come from several religious groups, as well as from individuals, denominations, and some Church leaders.

If we look back at what has been happening over these last few decades, we must admit that God in His sovereignty has been moving to prepare His Church for its great purpose and destiny.

How has this new move of God, commonly referred to as the New Apostolic Reformation, come about? Could it have been a progressive happening? Could God have been working progressively throughout history, in different times and different seasons, bringing revelation back to His Church? If we recall anything of Church history, I believe we would shout a resounding, "Yes!" God is a speaking, revealing God.

When I use the words, *progressive revelation,* I do not mean God is giving us new words of revelation that will become like new scriptures to us. What I clearly mean is that God is illuminating His Word, which is already in our Scripture, to us and that we are receiving a deeper and fuller understanding of what He is saying to the Church today.

He reminds us in Amos 3:7 that "Surely the Sovereign Lord does nothing without revealing his plan to his servants the prophets." God has always had His Prophets, but they have not always been recognized. This has resulted in their messages not being received. Nevertheless, He has been speaking; He has been revealing; He has been moving the Church toward its grand destiny for generations, in ever increasing measure. His revelation of His plan has been progressive, and He continues to pour out progressive revelation on us today.

Progressive Revelation

These two critical words, *progressive revelation,* are critical for us to understand and embrace. If we can truly grasp both the *definition* and the *implication* of these words—what they mean and what they do not mean—our ears will be open to hear what the Spirit is saying to the Church today. Furthermore, an accurate understanding of this term will silence much ungodly criticism that results from misinterpreting these words.

What Progressive Revelation is *Not*

Let me briefly make clear what progressive revelation is not. First, progressive revelation does not mean nor imply that a person is receiving some extra-biblical revelation that is "beyond" Scripture. Second, progressive revelation is not a revelation that is equal to Scripture or that would need to be added to Scripture. I firmly believe the canon of Scripture is closed and has been closed for thousands of years. Therefore, when I use the term "progressive revelation," I am not in any way advocating additions or adjustments to the Word of God.

When addressing some of the questions concerning the words *progressive revelation* in an article published in the November/December 2004 issue of *Ministries Today*, Peter Wagner offered a true and accurate assessment of Apostles who believe in progressive revelation and use the term. He wrote: "…the Apostles who I know, many of whom do receive revelation from God on a regular basis, would tremble at the thought that new truth that they receive would in any way violate the integrity and the authority of Scripture." I wholeheartedly agree.

Now that I have hopefully made my position clear, let's look at the positive and true understanding of what I and others mean when we talk about progressive revelation.

Progressive Revelation in Your Life

Let me begin with a very simple illustration to help demystify progressive revelation and put into perspective our understanding of God and His ways, which are never static. I am sure you can remember the moment you first accepted

Jesus Christ as your Lord and Savior. At that moment you had a "new revelation" of God. That experience, called "being born again," changed your life completely. The revelation of God's love, His power, and His desire to forgive your sin and rebellion caused you to feel that you could accept God and know Him.

At that moment, did you feel that you had received a great revelation, perhaps the ultimate revelation? If you are like many others in the wake of a salvation experience, you asked, "What else could there be?" Indeed. What else could there be? Because now you had received a revelation of God, and it produced such a powerful change in you. At last, you had wonderful joy, peace, and freedom as never before.

...when I use the term "progressive revelation," I am not in any way advocating additions or adjustments to the Word of God.

Now, let me ask you, since that encounter, do you understand God, salvation, holiness, the character of Christ, the power of His Holy Spirit, and His call upon your life more today than you did on the day you first prayed your prayer of repentance? I would dare to assume that your answer is "yes." Hmmmm. Could it be that you have progressed in your revelation of God, His nature, His heart, and His ways? This is just one simple example of what we mean when we speak of progressive revelation today.

Progressive Revelation Defined

Each of us has received progressive revelation in the areas I mentioned above—and in many other aspects of our faith—since we first received Jesus as Lord and Savior. God is continually revealing Himself to us and unfolding His plans and purposes progressively as we mature in Him. He has not shown us or "told" us everything yet, nor have we yet experienced everything He has for us. God still has more to say and give to His Church. Therefore, throughout the coming chapters we will see again and again that God has spoken to different generations, in different seasons, words I consider to be progressive revelation—unfolding plans for restoring His Church back to her original power and purpose. Progressive revelation takes place when God speaks prophetically a "now" word concerning another truth He wants to see functioning in His Church today, a divine truth that has always been in Scripture, but that we have failed to "see" or understand until now.

> *God is continually revealing Himself to us and unfolding His plans and purposes progressively as we mature in Him. He has not shown us or "told" us everything yet, nor have we yet experienced everything He has for us.*

Lest I leave the impression that progressive revelation is something new, let me reiterate that God has been sharing progressive revelation throughout Church history. In fact, progressive revelation has been part of the experience of God's people since the creation of man and throughout history. He has always been "on the move," and, in the next chapter, we will look at several examples of His progressive revelations to men and women.

CHAPTER 2

A God of Revelation

A QUICK OVERVIEW of the Old Testament shows us that God has always been revealing Himself progressively to His people. He did not give only one revelation about all His ways, His plans, or His nature. There was no one-time revelation that covered all aspects of God. Rather God's way has always been progressive revelation.

Adam and Eve

Beginning in the Garden of Eden, God revealed Himself to Adam and Eve. They heard directly from God concerning how they should live and which fruit they could and could not eat; yet He gave them dominion over everything else. When they disobeyed Him and ate of the "forbidden" fruit, they received a new revelation. Up until that time, Adam and Eve only had the revelation of God and His love, His protection, His provision, and His wisdom. Now they discovered that God was also a God of judgment for individual sin and rebellion. This was a new or progressive revelation at that time. Their understanding progressed beyond the previous revelation they had received.

Noah

When we look at Noah, we see that he was unique. He actually heard the voice of God sharing progressive revelation. God told Noah to build an ark, something no one had ever seen before. No one else on earth heard God speak progressive revelation, but Noah did.

From Noah's story we can learn that as leaders, we should not be influenced by circumstances or by other people. A leader knows when he or she has received new progressive revelation of what God wants to do, and he or she will obey God first, just as Noah obeyed God.

Noah not only received the revelation that God would judge individual sin, as in the case of Adam and Eve, he also experienced the revelation of God's judgment on corporate sin. God said, basically, "I will destroy every living thing with the flood, everything except Noah, his family, and the creatures in the ark." With each new season of God, there have always been leaders who hear directly from Him.

Abraham

Another example was when God told Abraham to leave his hometown of Ur. He said, "Abraham, I'll lead you to a new land." Although Abraham did not always make the best decisions, he endeavored to walk in obedience to the revelation he had received from God.

If you look into the Book of Genesis, God told Abraham to offer up his son, Isaac. A little bit later, as they are going up the mountain, God told Abraham, "Do not harm your son." Suddenly, Abraham was receiving a different word. I would not be surprised if he had responded, "But God, you just told me to offer up my son."

It is a good thing that Abraham did not live today. Some of us would have immediately begun to argue with God: "Hey God, first you promise me a son; then that son was so long in coming; then you told me to offer my son, which I was prepared to do. Now, I hear a voice telling me *not* to harm the boy. What is going on? I know, it must be the devil trying to distract me and cause me to miss God's spoken, revealed will for Isaac and me." Stop a moment; what do we learn here?

A leader knows when he or she has received new progressive revelation of what God wants to do, and he or she will obey God first, just as Noah obeyed God.

God gave Abraham different words at different times for different purposes. Think about this: What if Abraham had resisted God's "second" word? What if he had said, "God, you told me to offer my son. I really know that was your voice. Now, I am up here and ready to offer my son and here comes this voice that says, 'Do not harm him.' This cannot be your voice, God. It must be the devil speaking; he does not want me to obey you"?

What if Abraham had thought that way and not received the "second word" God spoke to him? You see, as leaders, it is important for us to maintain a daily intimate relationship with the Lord, so we will know His voice. God does not always repeat the same words of the past. God is a revealing God, thus He will speak today and give us a "now" word for His new season for the Church.

Once His word, that is, a "now" word is given, God will expect us to start walking in obedience to that "now" word. Often the problem is that our ears are still in tune to what God was saying yesterday or 20 years ago. When God gives us a new word, He also gives a new strategy. Let me make this clear: We can judge any new word we receive because no new word will ever violate the Word of God or the character of God.

You see, God did not want to kill Isaac, Abraham's son. God was testing Abraham. God wanted Abraham's heart, not his son. His heart. The same is true today. God wants our hearts—your heart and my heart.

David

In David's life we see another example of progressive revelation. God told David to ambush the Philistines. He said, "I will be with you." Later, on another occasion God said, "David, don't go after them." Was God confused? No. God simply gave David a different strategy for a different time.

From this, we can begin to understand how God works. If God knows the beginning from the end, then we must be open to what God was saying and doing yesterday, yet we must also be open to hear God's new strategy for the new battles of today and tomorrow. I believe God is a speaking God; He gives new strategies for each new season. Herein is a paradox; God never changes, yet God is always changing. There are many examples in Scripture where God "changed His mind" in response to prayer or in response to people when they repented. All we need to do is recall Jonah's message to the city of Nineveh and the story of Abraham when he interceded on behalf of Sodom and Gomorrah. We see that God was willing reverse the plan He originally announced.

There are things that God spoke in the past; He endorsed those things He said. He confirmed and even blessed the things He said. But those were "then" words; they were yesterday's words.

> *I believe God is a speaking God; He gives new strategies for each new season.*

God has not changed, but His word of progressive revelation to us does change with each of His new seasons. God wants to give us a today word, a "now" word. Thus, we must have an ear to hear what the Spirit is saying *now.*

We would all agree that God is up to something. It's a new season in the Kingdom of God. The future of the Church depends on you and me, the present-day leadership.

Is it possible for us to come to the point that we would say, if necessary: "I would be willing to sacrifice my thinking of yesterday. I would be willing to sacrifice my training. I would be willing to sacrifice my tradition and sacrifice my pre-conceived ideas, if necessary, in order to receive what God has for me now"?

Esther

Esther shows us another way in which we can receive progressive revelation. God positioned her in such a way that she could save her nation from destruction. In Esther's situation, she received God's revelation through Mordecai, her uncle. Still today, God can speak to us personally and directly, or He may choose to speak revelation to us through those who are older or have spiritual authority in our lives.

It was Mordecai who challenged Esther to rise up and use her new position and favor with the King for eternal purposes, to stop the destruction of an entire nation.

You might ask, "How in the world can a beauty queen save a nation?" Simple, God's ways are higher than our ways. He can use whomever He chooses. God will use any of us, if we will allow Him to do so.

Revelation, Obedience, Blessing

When we study Nehemiah and Daniel and many others throughout the Old Testament, we see that each of them received progressive revelation concerning God, His plans, and His ways. A principle we can learn is this: Revelation demands obedience, and obedience brings blessings. We need to remember that though revelation brings blessings, it also brings change. Embracing the changes God wants us to embrace, as the result of revelation, will open the door for blessings to come.

CHAPTER 3

The Church: Present and Past

ARE YOU AWARE THAT God is doing a new thing across the globe today? Yes, He is definitely shifting and changing many things in our world. Since this is true and our world is changing, the Church will also need to change, to experience a new paradigm—a new understanding of leadership and how that new leadership should function in God's Kingdom.

When we look at the world in which we live, we see that it is changing very fast—and the rate of change is accelerating with each passing day. Well-known Church researcher George Barna tells us in his book, *The Second Coming of the Church,* that our world is changing and re-inventing itself every 3 to 5 years. Barna goes on to say that the Church only adapts to change about every 30-50 years, and also emphasizes that "the church world has changed relatively little in the last half century" *(The Second Coming of the Church,* Nashville, TN: Thomas Nelson, Inc., 2001). This striking observation tells us that the Church is lagging far behind the world in many respects. We simply are not "seeing" and adjusting to the changes that are taking place in the world around us. This ought not to be.

As a result of the Church's failure to adapt to change many believers basically feel that the Church is only training and equipping them to do ministry within the four walls of their church buildings. They do not feel adequately equipped to do the works of ministry outside a physical church structure—at work, at the gym, in the neighborhood, or in social settings.

More alarming than that is the perception of the Church in the world at-large. Public opinion regards the Church as "backward" and out of touch. Many un-churched people view local churches as insular, isolated, and unaware of what is going on in the world. In other words, the world looks at the Church, and they see it as archaic. Society today feels the Church is distant and ignorant, that it does not understand the problems people are facing or the issues that matter to the average person. Often, the people in the communities around churches do not feel welcome or accepted in these churches. Citizens of the world look at the Church and see a museum —a place where outdated systems, methodologies, and programs exist for out-of-touch people. In addition, "ordinary people" do not see the Church as possessing much supernatural power. Therefore, they ask, since the Church is neither relevant to contemporary life nor understanding of the needs of people on earth, how can Church leaders and members be trusted in important, often life-changing, spiritual matters and issues?

Society today feels the Church is distant and ignorant, that it does not understand the problems people are facing or the issues that matter to the average person.

The realities to which I have just called your attention are shocking to many Christian leaders, and they create a gap that must be closed between Christianity and the cultures of this world. It is time for the Church to wake up and accept that we are behind when it comes to recognizing and adjusting to the changes taking place in both our physical world and in the spiritual realm—changes that increasingly cause the Church to end up farther and farther behind the cultures and societies in which they actually exist.

When we look around, we can see a world that is losing its moral moorings. We only need a casual reading of the Scriptures to be awakened to the realization that we are living in critical times. However, when we remember Barna's present-day statistics, we are confronted with a shocking reality: The Church is ill-equipped to rise to the level of spiritual warfare in which we are engaged today. If we are going to have the strength needed to stand against the forces of darkness that have been unleashed in this generation, we must have change—and it must begin with our leaders.

As I mentioned in the introduction, there are more churches in our world today than ever before. If you look at the various statistics available, you will find that there are more Christians in the world today than in all of time past. These facts call for a question: "With more churches and more people calling themselves Christians than ever before, why do we see sin abounding, society going downhill, and wars and famine increasing?" All of this should signal something to us. There is a desperate need for change, and I say again, it must begin with the leadership of the Church.

When we look into Scripture, we find Paul's instruction concerning the biblical paradigm for leadership—a paradigm that is now being restored to the structure of the Church universal and to local church bodies. As leaders, we need to have open minds toward change and toward the restoration of God's "Ascension gifts" back into the Church. This includes a shift in our understanding of how leadership in the Church should function. It calls for a return to the biblical principles that empowered the early Church to reach their world with the life-changing message of Jesus Christ.

Where Did We Go Wrong?

Could it be that we are trapped in a form of religion, a form of righteousness, but we have lost the power available to us in our faith? Could it be that we, the Church, are "resting on our laurels" while we are locked in outdated structures and leadership functions? Have we fallen into religious passivity? Is it possible that God is speaking progressive revelation to us today, telling us that we need to stop producing "managers" in the Church and begin to identify and empower five-fold leaders in the Body of Christ, leaders who can make a difference in the world and for the Kingdom of God?

> *If we are going to have the strength needed to stand against the forces of darkness that have been unleashed in this generation, we must have change—and it must begin with our leaders.*

A Progressive God

God is a progressive God; we must always remember this. Through the generations, He has brought progressive revelation to His Church. Through progressive revelation, He brought the Church out of the Dark Ages, and yet we are still struggling with some of the damage done to the Church during this period of history. Let me explain.

Recorded Church history tells us that for 300 years prior to the Dark Ages, the early Church had been growing and impacting nations, even though Christianity was considered illegal.

We read in the Book of Acts that the early Church gathered in small groups and met in homes. In these homes, people prayed for one another; they were accountable to one another; and they cared for one another. Both men and women, ordinary believers, served as leaders of these small groups. They experienced true, accountable covenant relationships. For 300 years after the birth of the Church—through these house groups—early believers successfully took the message of Jesus Christ to the nations of the earth. Then history took a dramatic turn.

The Emperor Constantine

In 313 A.D., the Emperor Constantine had a dream in the night. In that dream, he saw a cross and words across the sky. The words said: "In this sign, conquer." Constantine made a cross and fought a very significant battle the next day. He won the battle. Those two experiences changed his heart about Christianity, and he issued a decree that made Christianity a legal religion. This brought an end to the persecution of Christians, and they began to enjoy peace and political prosperity.

Immediately, many aspects of Christianity changed. People no longer needed to "believe" in Christ or have a personal experience with God to be called a Christian; all they needed to do was to sign up. To encourage people, those who "signed up" to be Christians did not have to fight in the army or pay taxes. Naturally, these were good incentives for people to declare that they were Christians. As a result, the spiritual life of the Church began to deteriorate.

By 323 A.D., Constantine began to build large church buildings throughout the Roman Empire. People then abandoned the small house groups led by lay people and began to meet in large "holy buildings" under the leadership of a "holy man."

How the Dark Ages Affected Church Leadership

These changes under the Emperor Constantine meant that people no longer developed a personal relationship with Christ or accountable relationships with one another. Leadership changed (this is where the ministry of lay people—both men and women—was snuffed out); accountability shifted; and the spiritual life of the Church disintegrated. Later, the letters of Peter, Paul, Mark, James, and John were collected and put into what we now call our canonized Bible. At this same time, the canonized Bible was only available in Latin, which meant that the holy writings were no longer available to the ordinary person. Only the holy man who could read Latin in the holy building had access to God's Word.

Lay people (non-clergy) stopped doing the "works of ministry." Therefore, if people needed someone to pray for them, they had to call the holy man. If they wanted to know something about God or to find out what the Word of God said, then they had to go to the holy building and find a holy man who understood Latin. With these developments, the entire structure of the Church—church government; who can minister, who cannot; who can pray, and who cannot; who can hear from God and who cannot—was redefined, and the Church entered into a period called the Dark Ages.

This period lasted from the fifth century until the fifteenth century—1000 years. No wonder the Church has struggled to break free from the influence of the Dark Ages; it is deeply ingrained in our history.

Since the Dark Ages, the Church has never been the same.

During the Dark Ages, many religious symbols and relics were introduced. People demanded objects, pictures, candles, statues, images, and similar items to represent the God with whom they no longer had a personal relationship—because they wanted some way to be able to "touch" or connect with Him. Since the Dark Ages, the Church has never been the same.

CHAPTER 4

The Need for a New Wineskin

IN MANY WAYS, THE Church today is still locked in the Dark Ages. Though time and technology have moved us beyond the official time period by that name, ~~much of our modern-day thinking about local church structure came from the Dark Ages,~~ not from the early church. Some of the doctrine we still embrace came from the Dark Ages. When we look closely, our concepts of leadership—who can lead and how leaders function—also comes from the distorted view of the Church and the approach to leadership that was developed during the Dark Ages.

Even some of our divisive traditions came from the Dark Ages. For example, the removal of women from ministry, to the point of forbidding their obedience to God, came from the Dark Ages, not from God's Word. Our emphasis on the need for holy buildings also came from this unfortunate time in history. In fact, most of our current thinking and ideas about leadership, purpose, and structure in the local church—including the virtual elimination of Apostles and Prophets in leadership roles—has come from the Dark Ages, not from Scripture. Overall, the impact of the Dark Ages weakened the Church, replacing much of its vitality and strength with ritual, legalism, and forms of religion that were absent of power.

Four Key Words

I believe there are four words that clearly describe to us what God is doing today and why—how He is changing His Church and bringing us into the new seasons and structures He has for us. It begins with *revelation*, which results in reformation. *Reformation* then produces *restoration* (of a divine truth that has been lost to the Church). As truth is restored, it results in *transformation* that takes us back to God's original intended purpose.

This process is a process of change; it is a process of progressive revelation. When we pray, "Our Father...Your Kingdom come, Your will be done, on earth as it is in heaven," what are we asking for? We are asking for transformation to take place on earth, so earth will be aligned with the plan and purposes of God's Kingdom.

However, for change to take place, it must first take place in the leadership of the Church. If we, the leaders, close our ears and harden our hearts, we will reap a different harvest.

When God begins to lead us into a new season and Church leadership does not receive His progressive revelation, but instead, the people begin to hear the voice of God's Spirit releasing His new season, what happens? Then the people will openly and with great hunger embrace what God is saying; their hearts will begin to change as they begin to experience God at a new level. Simply stated—if the people change before the leadership changes, we will have *revolution,* not reformation! Another way to say it is this: We arrive at reformation the hard way.

No one wants a revolution; we should all desire reformation. Know this: Reformation is usually "radical." We, the Pastors and leaders of the Church, must receive God's progressive

> *...if the people change before the leadership changes, we will have revolution, not reformation!*

revelation concerning His time and new season for us today. Thus, it is imperative that we know how to confront and embrace change. We cannot continue in the old wineskins (old mindsets).

Revelation and Old Wineskins

When Jesus taught that new wine could not be put into old wineskins, He was saying that it would not work unless the old wineskins were transformed and made open and flexible like the new wineskins. Only then could they receive the new wine.

If we are "old wineskins" and God tries to pour the "new wine" of His Spirit into us, then the dynamics, robust activity, stirring, and movement of the new wine will cause the old skins to burst, break, and be destroyed. Jesus makes very clear that old wineskin structures simply cannot take the changes He is introducing. God is wanting new wineskins, new structures that can hold His new wine.

Does this mean the old wineskins were bad? Of course not. The old wineskins were God-given. In practical terms, this means we must not be critical of our heritage. Good old wineskin structures in the Church served their purposes for their generation. They were valuable and anointed for effectiveness in their seasons. Now, it is God's time for new wine to be poured forth for a new generation.

Revelation Brings Reformation

God has always given revelation to those who seek it. In many instances, these revelations have brought reformation to the Church—reformation that continues to this day as God restores His strong and

God is wanting new wineskins, new structures that can hold His new wine.

victorious Church. While God has used a number of men and women to move His Church toward more and more reformation, I want to mention several people specifically and call your attention to their outstanding accomplishments.

Martin Luther

Many Church historians accept the year 1517 A.D. as the official beginning of Church reformation. In that year, a significant and "Church-changing" revelation came to a man by the name of Martin Luther, a German priest and professor of theology. In an act commonly regarded as the beginning of the period of Church history known as "The Reformation," Martin Luther nailed his *95 Theses* on the door of the Castle Church in Wittenberg. God's progressive revelation had broken into his heart, and the Holy Spirit brought fresh revelation from Romans 3:22; "The just shall live by faith." Suddenly, he understood that people could go to God directly in prayer, without having to go through a priest.

Luther's work began a revival of interest in the Word of God and a return to biblical principles throughout the Church. It shifted the focus of Christians away from the holy church buildings and the holy men, away from ritual to reality. This was what I call a "new wineskin" revelation for Luther. God was speaking progressive revelation.

The Wesley Brothers

In the 17th century England, John and Charles Wesley, John Knox, and George Whitefield were used mightily by God to bring further progressive revelation to the Church. The Wesleyan Holiness movement was birthed during this time, in which we saw the restoration of the priesthood of the believer, a renewed commitment to holiness, and a fresh emphasis on personal relationship with God.

John Wesley trained believers in the Word of God and sent trained lay preachers out all over the country. Believers began to meet again in small groups, just as they had in the Book of Acts. This was the restoration of lay people doing the "work of the ministry"—the ministry of reconciliation. The Apostle Paul writes of this in 2 Corinthians 5:18-20.

Under Wesley's influence, people began to live and experience something called "covenant relationship." They called one another to accountability and holy living. Wesley even allowed women to be involved in ministry, saying, "Her gifts and anointing will make a way for her." These were all aspects of Christian life that had been lost during the Dark Ages. Again we see progressive revelation bringing reformation to the Church.

Thank God, He is bringing the Church progressively out of the bondage of the Dark Ages into the restoration of the things He has desired and designed for the Church since its earliest days.

The Pentecostals

The 1900's saw the birth of the Pentecostal movement, in which the gifts of the Holy Spirit were evident much like they were in the Book of Acts. God began to demonstrate in remarkable ways that He was alive and that He was still a powerful, healing, prayer-answering God. This was a fresh releasing of first-century manifestations of God's Holy Spirit and power—and it was yet another stride in progressive revelation.

As had happened in other seasons of progressive revelation, this era introduced new language to the Church. Phrases such as "baptism in the Holy Spirit," "speaking in tongues," "laying on of hands," and "slain in the Spirit" became part of the vernacular in many churches as God's people entered into new progressive revelation. Each new revelation in God's restoration process has required us to dig into the Word of God and seek wisdom and understanding of His revelation. It is easier to receive revelation than it is to mature in knowing what to do with the revelation we receive.

The Great Evangelists

In the 1940's and 1950's, the Church had Billy Graham, Oral Roberts, and T.L. Osborne, plus many other great revivalists and healing evangelists. During these years we saw the modern-day restoration and widespread acceptance of the office of the Evangelist.

The Prayer Movement

In the 1970's and 1980's, a renewed emphasis on prayer began to take shape. New types of prayer, new levels of prayer, and a whole new vocabulary for prayer began to materialize, and a movement focused heavily on intercession emerged.

During this time, the Church also began to receive greater understanding about spiritual warfare. We learned how to pray more effectively against Satan and his schemes. This was part of the restoration of prayer, with a clear understanding of its important role in the Church and the life of the believer. During the emphasis on intercession and spiritual warfare, God was restoring the prayer dimension of His power to the Church.

Ongoing Restoration

Each of the movements I have mentioned in this chapter is an important milestone for us to see and understand so we are not afraid of the words *revelation* and *restoration.* Everything I have highlighted, from Martin Luther's *95 Theses* in 1571 through the 1970's and beyond, has restored yet another component of God's truth concerning His Church and its ministries—truths that were lost during the Dark Ages.

Thank God, He is bringing the Church progressively out of the bondage of the Dark Ages into the restoration of the things He has desired and designed for the Church since its earliest days. Truly, He is using progressive revelation to provide the Church with strength to stand in the midst of the physical and spiritual pressures of our day. Remember: Revelation brings reformation; reformation brings restoration; and restoration brings transformation.

CHAPTER 5

Restoration Today

THE APOSTLE PAUL began sharing progressive revelation concerning God's new order in 1 Corinthians 12:28, when he wrote: "And in the church God has appointed first of all apostles, second prophets, third teachers, then...." This was an entirely new paradigm for spiritual leadership of the Church, both in his day and now, in ours.

Prior to this, God's people derived their main understanding of spiritual leadership from the forms followed in the tabernacle priesthood, worship in the Temple, a sacrificial system using animals, and daily life governed by the Law.

Then Jesus came along and introduced a new structure called "My Church" (see Matthew 16:18), but He did not personally offer much detail on how leadership would function in His new structure. Only later, when the Apostle Paul began to share the progressive revelation he had received on the back side of the Arabian desert, concerning order, structure, and leadership related to the five-fold ministry offices, could we come to better understand the new leadership titles, functions, and responsibilities.

A Kingdom Purpose

God has a Kingdom purpose in the restoration of His five-fold ministry gifts and in the progressive revelation He continues to give us concerning these offices. His purpose is not to just give people titles or greater authority in order to exalt men and women or to build their personal kingdoms. Rather, God's purpose is that His Kingdom might be established and His leadership, function, and structure for local church government might be restored within the body of Christ. The Church will then function in His way, with His anointing, to rule and reign with Him.

You read in the previous chapter: *Revelation* brings *reformation;* and *reformation* results in *restoration* (of God's truth) in order for *transformation* to take place. This process will bring about God's new order for the Church and result in the answer to our prayer, "…Your Kingdom come, your will be done, on earth as it is in heaven." This becomes reality when the kingdoms of this world are transformed to become the kingdoms of our God.

Transformation, the ushering in of His Kingdom to every sphere of life and society, cannot find full expression until we first define how God's new order will function as full restoration takes place. One thing is certain: His new order will first demand new paradigms for leadership.

A Great Destiny

God's Church has—and has always had—a great and glorious destiny, and though it seems slow at times, we are moving into that calling and purpose as never before. However, let me reiterate that I believe the destiny of the Church can only be fully realized as God's leaders rise up and take their proper place in the Church.

From the beginning of time, God has anointed and appointed leaders to accomplish His purposes on earth. He did so with Moses, Joshua, David, the Twelve Apostles, Paul, and others. His *modus operandi* of using leaders to fulfill His plan has not changed. Don't look now, but He is still working through His leaders today.

Historically, the Church has been through phases when some leadership positions were more visible and more widely accepted than others. But now we live in a day when all of the five-fold ministry, the leadership structure of the Church

God's purpose is that His Kingdom might be established and His leadership, function, and structure for local church government might be restored within the body of Christ.

listed in Ephesians 4:11—Apostles, Prophets, Evangelists Pastors, and Teachers—has been restored. As the five-fold leaders emerge and minister in the offices to which God has called them, the Church will increasingly fulfill God's plan and function in levels of authority and effectiveness that have always been in His heart, but have yet to be recognized fully on earth.

The Five-fold Ministry

God has designed the five-fold ministry as the leadership structure and the leadership team for the Church, and He has given these offices to the Church as a gift. Ephesians 4:11, 12 makes this clear: "It was he [Christ] who *gave* some to be apostles, some to be prophets, some to be evangelists, and some to be pastors and teachers, to prepare God's people for works of service, so that the body of Christ may be built up" (emphasis mine).

The first responsibility of five-fold ministers is to serve—to serve God by serving the Church and to serve one another and God's people in such a way that their strengths combine to edify and build up the Church. This working together is essential for His Church to stand strong in the days in which we live and to make the impact that He intends it to make in today's world.

Each of the five-fold offices has different anointings and expressions, and we need them all. No one person can offer everything the body of Christ needs, so we need teamwork within the five-fold ministry. The reason we have been given five offices, and not one or two, is that we need a variety of anointings, giftings, and perspectives to contribute and work together for the strengthening of the Church. The anointings and expressions within the five-fold ministry work together, in mutual submission and cooperation to edify the body of Christ and to help the Church mature.

> *God has designed the five-fold ministry as the leadership structure and the leadership team for the Church, and He has given these offices to the Church as a gift.*

The Value of Titles

People often ask me if titles are important in ministry, especially in regard to five-fold ministers. While a title certainly does not "make" a person an Apostle, Prophet, Pastor, Teacher, or Evangelist, I do believe titles serve several important purposes in the Church when they are used appropriately and received with humility by people who deserve them.

Let me explain. First, titles are valuable in the Church today because they communicate a leader's functions, responsibilities, and obligations; they help a group or congregation know what to expect from that leader. The clear expectations titles communicate will help a church or ministry run smoothly.

Second, titles position leaders properly because they communicate the measure of authority a leader has within an organization. When spheres and levels of authority are understood, leadership can function much more effectively.

Third, titles help people receive leaders in their respective anointings. When people know what a leader's office and anointing is, they can receive the blessings that accompany that office and anointing. For example, if a Prophet is scheduled to speak in a church service, those who attend will be prepared for a prophetic anointing and flow, and if they have been taught well, they will know how to receive that message as a prophetic word and how to judge that word. Similarly, a congregation can receive a Teacher as one who has come primarily to share biblical truth, and they can receive a Pastor as one who loves and cares for them as a shepherd does for his flock.

Much confusion can be avoided and much blessing can be released in our churches today if we will simply begin to receive ministers in the offices and anointings God has given them. The proper use of titles will help us accomplish that purpose.

For more detailed information on the use of titles in five-fold ministry, please see my book, *Commissioning: The Process, Protocol, and Importance of Commissioning Modern-Day Apostles.*

Bringing Clarity to Confusion

As I have noted, you and I are currently witnessing the full restoration of the five-fold ministry, especially the restoration of the office of the Apostle. As we are seeing the full restoration of all the five-fold ministries, the Church is also experiencing some confusion. This should not cause us to be afraid to embrace God's new order, but rather to recognize that during a time of restoration there is also a corresponding time of "confusion" as the new things are coming into proper alignment. It can be confusing; but it is also exciting.

Roles, Functions, and Characteristics

Part of the restoration underway in the Church today involves defining the characteristics and functions of Apostles, communicating their roles in the modern-day Church, and educating believers about how to receive and relate to Apostles. I will address these issues in greater detail in Section II of this book, but for now I simply want to call attention to it as an area of confusion that must be dealt with.

Much confusion can be avoided and much blessing can be released in our churches today if we will simply begin to receive ministers in the offices and anointings God has given them.

Language

Across the board, we are also seeing confusion in terminology. For instance, we use the words *apostolic* and *Apostle* as though they have identical meanings. Usually, this is the result of a fear to actually call someone an Apostle. Naturally, it is safer and less controversial to say they are "apostolic." The same is true for the word *prophetic* and *Prophet.*

Local Church Implications

Finally, I want to address some of the confusion that has come into local churches and local church leaders as the restoration of the five-fold ministry continues to unfold.

As the restoration of Apostles and Prophets has progressed, some Pastors and church leaders have become concerned because they have experienced some confusion in their own roles as leaders, and/or their congregations have become confused as they have learned about the restoration that is taking place without being trained and equipped to recognize and understand the roles, functions, character traits, and mindsets associated with each of the five-fold offices.

Many local church Pastors are not sure where they "fit" in the restoration process. They are not opposed to acknowledging Apostles and Prophets, but since they only understand their present role as Pastor, they are not sure how to relate to these newly-restored governmental offices, especially when they begin to hear talk about the "power" and "authority" of Apostles and Prophets. Many have begun to wonder what will happen if they discover they are really an Apostle or a Prophet in a Pastor's "skin" or with a Pastor's title.

During the beginning of this restoration, some Pastors began to quickly acknowledge or assume, "I am an Apostle," or "I am a Prophet." Then, they suddenly "ejected" from the local church and hit the road to "ordain" other people into the office of Apostle and Prophet. This has not been beneficial to the Church or to the restoration movement.

I am sure we would all agree that we can often receive revelation but not have full understanding of what to do with it. Thus, because of a lack of understanding and teaching in areas of character, protocol, function, responsibility, relationships, and accountability, we began to hear of problems such as: abuse of power, pride, lack of accountability, and especially the lack of working relationships between Apostles and Prophets. These unfortunate situations have caused some Christian leaders to "throw out the baby with the bath water." This is an urgent area of concern.

I believe God desires all Pastors and denominational leaders to be open to "hear what the Spirit is saying" to the Church today. As we hear His voice, let us remove every barrier that would hinder us from receiving God's progressive revelation for the 21st century. He is revealing and restoring to us His design for the five-fold ministry as the leadership structure of the Church. He is calling us to embrace the changes that are necessary for the Church to become a strong, effective, vital, and victorious force upon the earth. For this to happen, we must make room for the leadership gifts of Apostles and Prophets to function.

> *I believe God desires all Pastors and denominational leaders to be open to "hear what the Spirit is saying" to the Church today.*

Section II:

The Apostolic Ministry

CHAPTER 6

Understanding Apostles and Apostolic Leadership

FOR THE CHURCH TO continue to gain strength to stand in this difficult hour, apostolic leadership must arise. I am not calling for leaders to simply function apostolically, but for true Apostles to step into their God-given offices throughout the Body of Christ. The leadership of Apostles, along with the leadership of the other five-fold ministry gifts, will equip the Church for impact in our day.

Before we continue in this chapter, let me clarify what I mean by the word *apostolic* and what I mean by the word *Apostle.* First, *apostolic* is an adjective; it is one word that describes another word. We might say that a person has an "apostolic mindset;" that there is an "apostolic structure" in a church, network, or organization; that someone has an "apostolic approach" to ministry or business, or an "apostolic strategy" for church or business growth. This word can be used to modify a variety of other words or phrases.

The word *Apostle,* on the other hand, refers to an individual—a specific man or woman who is called and anointed by God for the five-fold office which bears this name. All believ-

> *All believers should be apostolic, which in its most basic sense means, "sent" to do God" work, but not all believers are to serve God's people as Apostles.*

ers should be apostolic, which in its most basic sense means, "sent to do God's work," but not all believers are to serve God's people as Apostles. Similarly, all believers should be prophetic—able to hear the voice of God—but not all believers are Prophets.

True Apostles operate in many ways in God's Kingdom—both in spiritual and in business arenas. They also serve in many capacities, accomplish great works, and carry out a multitude of responsibilities in the spheres of influence to which God has assigned them.

But works and functions alone do not make a person an Apostle. Apostles must also demonstrate character traits that are consistent with godly apostolic ministry; they need to exhibit thought processes that distinguish them from other five-fold ministers; and they must produce fruit that affirms their apostleship. When we identify Apostles, we must take a holistic approach. We must not attempt to identify them simply by function, work, personal magnetism, or natural gifting, but we also need to keep in mind other critical areas such as character, mindset, and ministry results.

Apostles or Spiritual Mothers and Fathers?

Before we delve into understanding who Apostles are and what they do, I want to make clear that Apostles are *not* necessarily spiritual mothers and fathers. While we have a great need in the body of Christ for "mothers" and "fathers" in the faith, Apostles do not fill these roles, in the strictest sense.

Let me explain. Many believers have a "spiritual Mom" and/or a "spiritual Dad." These are people who have cared about our spiritual development and helped us mature in our faith. These people can be likened to natural parents—those who make sure children have lunch money and shoes that fit, and who make sure their immunizations are up-to-date. They pay attention to details in their children's lives, set the rules of the household, meet physical, emotional, and relational needs of their children, and provide encouragement and support for their lives.

Extended families, and some immediate families, not only have mothers and fathers, they also have matriarchs and patriarchs. These are people who have positions of great authority and respect, whose roles could be considered "governmental" in a family or tribe. Matriarchs and patriarchs are not nearly as concerned about immunizations and daily details as parents are. Rather, they are extremely concerned about the destinies of their descendants, about where their sons and daughters are headed in life, and about making sure they have the experiences and equipment to get there.

These matriarchs and patriarchs are not busy trying to establish themselves in their own careers or ministries (as many young parents are), but are intensely focused on those who will still be making an impact after they themselves have passed away. They are

> *In God's Kingdom, Apostles function primarily as matriarchs and patriarchs.*

doing everything they can to help their descendants succeed because they have already achieved measures of success in various areas, and their success now lies in the grooming and launching of other people's destinies.

In God's Kingdom, Apostles function primarily as matriarchs and patriarchs. This is not to say that they cannot also be spiritual mothers and fathers, but their main concern is the future of "the family" (the body of Christ) and the destinies of the individuals to whom they relate.

Generals in God's Army

As a starting point for a fuller understanding of Apostles and the apostolic ministry, let's examine the history of Apostles, starting in Jesus' day, and explore how they function today.

Apostles function in God's Kingdom as generals do in the military—at the highest levels of authority and strategy. Apostles must also have people who follow them, not in a legalistic sense but by virtue of their excellent leadership. For these reasons, the military analogy is appropriate in regard to Apostles and their ministries.

The Greek word translated *apostle* in English means quite simply, "sent one." However, the term acquired a broader meaning during the time of the Roman Empire. In those days, "apostles" were military generals who were chosen and sent as official emissaries from a government or an empire to conquer a new territory. After gaining victory over a region and its people, one of the generals' assignments was to teach the conquered people the language, customs, values, and ways of the conquering kingdom, the new kingdom to which those people now belonged. I believe we can look at the role of these generals in history and conclude that those who are chosen to function as Apostles of God's Kingdom should function in similar ways.

Jesus understood that the people in His day were familiar

with apostles who operated as generals in the military and political realms, as I have described. I believe this is one of the main reasons He introduced the word *apostle* to the Church as a title to describe leaders in His Kingdom (see Luke 6:13). When we realize what meant so many centuries ago, we can see that it is an accurate and appropriate word to describe the ministry of modern-day Apostles. Apostles today function in much the same way as apostles did in New Testament times—they are sent from God's Kingdom into enemy territory to subdue and to teach His Kingdom ways to those living in the kingdoms of this world.

> *Apostles function in God's Kingdom as generals do in the military—at the highest levels of authority and strategy.*

Apostles also function "militarily" in ways similar to military generals because they have been given great spiritual authority and have God-given anointings and graces to fight spiritual battles on the highest levels. Finally, the parallels between generals and Apostles continue when we realize that Apostles are set into office just as military generals are—by the process of commissioning. (For more on the commissioning of Apostles, please see my book, *Commissioning.*)

In the days when kings and emperors sent out apostles with military assignments, those "sent ones" identified the leader by whose authority they had been sent. For example, an apostle sent to conquer a territory and assimilate the people into the customs and language of the Roman Empire might say something to this effect: "I am Julius. I am sent by Caesar, and I come in his authority."

As we read the letters of the Apostles Paul and Peter, we see that the same applies to New Testament Apostles. Paul's greeting in his letter to the Galatians reads: "Paul, an apostle not from men nor through man, but through Jesus Christ and God the Father who raised Him from the dead" (Galatians 1:1, NKJV) and his greeting to the believers at Colossae reads: "Paul, an apostle of Jesus Christ by the will of God" (Colossians 1:1, NKJV). Similarly, Peter identifies himself as: "Peter, an apostle of Jesus Christ" in his first epistle (1 Peter 1:1, NKJV) and as: "Peter, a bondservant and apostle of Jesus Christ" in his second (2 Peter 1:1, NKJV).

Likewise, modern-day Apostles are chosen by God; they are sent according to His will; and they minister in His authority.

Apostolic Authority

To truly understand apostolic leadership, we must understand spheres of authority.

As I have written already, Apostles have tremendous authority in the spiritual realm, the highest level and greatest measure of spiritual authority available. But, we must realize that spiritual authority and earthly authority are not the same. Apostles only have authority on earth in the sphere where people have "given" them authority. In other words, Apostles only have apostolic authority in a church, city, or region where people recognize them as Apostles and are willing to follow them.

...modern-day Apostles are chosen by God; they are sent according to His will; and they minister in His authority.

A sphere of authority is not based on geography or territory; it is based on people, and it is based on relationships. The true evidence of a sphere of authority in an Apostle's ministry is not found in buildings or strategies, but people. The Apostle Paul wrote to the believers in Corinth: "....For *you are the seal of my apostleship in the Lord*" (1 Corinthians 9:2, italics mine). Real results are seen in an Apostle's ministry by the number of people who have been impacted, saved, changed, built up, and released to serve and lead—and who are willing to follow that person and say, "So-and-so is my Apostle." If a person is a true Apostle, he or she must have a following—a sphere of authority.

The Apostle Paul understood this, which is why he wrote to the believers in Corinth: "Even though I may not be an apostle to others, surely I am to you!" (1 Corinthians 9:2). What was Paul saying? He was making it clear that some people did not receive him as an Apostle; thus, he was not an Apostle to them. He was certainly an Apostle to the church in Corinth, but he was not received as an Apostle to the church in Rome. He had no sphere of authority in Rome because he did not have a group of followers there. However, we see that he had great spiritual authority in Corinth and in other cities.

As a modern-day example, let's say a man named John lives in the United States, but travels to Africa and is commissioned there as an Apostle. Should he then expect to be received as Apostle everywhere he goes? No, Apostles are only received as such—and can only exercise their spiritual authority—in their spheres of influence. If John were to go to Latin America after being recognized as an Apostle in Africa, he is only a guest or a visitor, and he should not try to operate as an Apostle there, unless they also choose to recognize him as an Apostle.

If he returns to the United States and tells people there that he was recognized as an Apostle in Africa, how will they react? They will say, "Well maybe you are an Apostle to them, but we have not acknowledged you. Therefore, you have no sphere of authority with us."

In a case such as I have just described, John would have a title, but no sphere of influence in which to operate. Therefore, he would have no true authority in the U.S. or Latin America.

It is important to understand that all Apostles, like Paul and the person I have just described, will be Apostles to some people, but not to everyone. This is why we need all types of Apostles in all spheres of influence to arise today. The release of heaven's authority on earth through Apostles is critical in times of spiritual warfare, and it is vital to the strengthening of the Church. I believe that the wise and proper use of apostolic authority is one of the reasons the Church is taking back territories from the enemy. This may be happening more slowly than we would like to see, but it is happening. As we grow in our understanding of spheres of authority and of apostolic authority, we will see this increase, and we will see God's Church grow stronger and stronger, with real strength to stand.

CHAPTER 7

How Apostles Function

EACH FIVE-FOLD MINISTRY office is unique. Each one requires certain strengths and giftings; each has its own anointing; each is characterized by distinct values, mindsets, and approaches to ministry; and each offers something vitally important to the body of Christ. We must not restrict the functions of any one office to the point that we say, for instance, "Prophets only prophesy" or "Teachers only teach," because Pastors and Evangelists can also teach and/or prophesy and Prophets, Apostles, or Teachers can—and often do—fill pastoral roles or work in the arena of evangelism. So, when we consider how Apostles operate in the body of Christ and in the world, we are not in any way excluding other offices or ministries from these same functions. At the same time, simply because a certain function does not appear in one Apostle's ministry, we are not to conclude that other Apostles cannot work in that particular way.

One of the common perceptions about Apostles today is that they plant churches. While many Apostles do establish new churches, we must resist the temptation to think that all Apostles plant churches and that all church planters are Apostles. This is the kind of old traditional thinking that will prevent the full spectrum of the apostolic ministry from being restored and released in our day. In the twenty-first century, we are realizing that Apostles function in many ways. Apostles do much more than plant churches, and they minister in many more ways than I can mention in this volume.

However, there are several books I would like to recommend as resources that will help you understand Apostles and their functions. Many of these books were written before the shift in language from "ordination" to "commissioning," but they still provide excellent insights into apostolic ministry.

- *Spheres of Authority: Apostles in Today's Church* by C. Peter Wagner (Wagner Publications)
- *Apostles and Prophets: the Foundation of the Church* by C. Peter Wagner (Wagner Publications)
- *Apostles and the Emerging Apostolic Movement* by David Cannistraci (Renew Books [a division of Gospel Light])
- *Leadershift: Transitioning from the Pastoral to the Apostolic* by John Eckhardt (Crusaders Ministries)

Apostles Think Differently

Much variety exists in the values people express and the perspectives and mindsets they hold as they approach their ministries, offices, anointings, or gifts. This is certainly true for five-fold ministers. Apostles think differently than Pastors, who think differently than Prophets, Teachers, and Evangelists—and vice versa in every situation.

In April 2003, Jim Hodges, an outstanding modern-day Apostle and I were sitting beside each other in a meeting chaired by Peter Wagner. During a break, I shared with Jim some thoughts about Apostles and leadership. Later, he shared with me (and subsequently with the entire group) a newsletter he had recently sent to all of the churches in his network. In it, he highlighted some of the differences he sees between Apostles and Pastors.

He had given considerable thought to these differences. At

While many Apostles do establish new churches, we must resist the temptation to think that all Apostles plant churches and that all church planters are Apostles.

that same time, I had been working on a list which would include not only Apostles and Pastors, but also included the "thinking" of the Prophet.

I call these distinctions to your attention to prove and to emphasize that no one gift is more important than the others. On the contrary, these distinctions will help us understand how much we really do need each other. This is why Jesus gave us the five—to emphasize that all the gifts must honor each other and work together.

The chart below shows what I have concluded from my observations of these three ministry gifts. This chart is by no means exclusive or prescriptive, and everything on it does not necessarily apply to every person who occupies the office being described. It is simply a reflection of general observations of common characteristics of Apostles, Prophets, and Pastors.

Prophets	Pastors	Apostles
Want their people in communion (connoting intimacy with God)	Want people in fellowship (connoting relationships with one another)	Want people on the battlefield (connoting warfare against the devil)
Are very comfortable with Apostles	Are very comfortable with Teachers	Are very comfortable with Prophets
Want to stir	Want to maintain	Want to expand
Want to nurture	Want to encourage	Want to build
Want to "shake the house"	Want to "keep house"	Want to "clean house"
Inspire	Settle	Pioneer
Want to change the course	Want to stay the course	Want to map the course
Tend to be creative	Tend to be managerial	Tend to be visionary
Issue calls for battle	Focus on logistics for battle	Focus on strategy for battle
Will see the vision	Want to maintain the vision	Want to empower for the vision
More functional	More stationary	More mobile
Focus on the throne of God	Focus on people	Focus on leaders
Want to experience the work	Want to oversee the work	Want to establish a work
Challenge	Comfort	Confront
Reveal the way	Care for people along the way	Lead the way
Anoint people	Assign people	Appoint people
See church as a place of intimacy with God	See church as a place for healing	See church as a battlefield
See God's will	Help people find God's will	Want to enforce God's will
Lead in travail	Lead through the veil	Lead to prevail

While we can see some humor in the different thought processes and approaches to ministry, it is very important that we do not think that one way of thinking is superior to the other. They are all important, and their differences are important. Again, differences help show us why we need all of the gifts and offices working together.

As we consider these distinctions, we can see that it is possible to discern identifying characteristics of a particular mindset in a person's ministry. While these characteristics are not conclusive in and of themselves, if a person exhibits a majority of them and aligns with other qualities, functions, and character traits mentioned in this book, it is very possible that he or she is anointed and called as an Apostle.

Key Functions of Apostles

Several important functions of true Apostles include:
- identifying and implementing changes needed to help advance God's purposes in individuals, churches, organizations, or geographical regions.
- working as master builders and strategists. Apostles are not satisfied with maintaining, but are always moving forward with strategies to build, strengthen, and expand, taking back territory from satan.
- making strategic decisions and taking responsibility for those decisions.
- operating in tremendous spiritual authority and serving as "generals" at the highest levels of spiritual warfare. Apostles also have the authority to war for territories.
- confronting heresy with great strength and power, always with the aim of bringing correction, restoration,

and alignment with God's ways and purposes.

- empowering others and launching people's destinies.
- functioning as pioneers, blazing new trials, breaking new ground, opening new territories, and leading the way for others to follow.
- functioning as ministers of revelation and impartation. In other words, they teach and preach in ways that bring spiritual understanding to their listeners, and they are able to stir up spiritual gifts inside of people.
- resolving conflicts and solving problems. They look for the "bottom line" as they identify and resolve issues.
- judging matters without being judgmental.

The functions mentioned above are intended to help explain how Apostles function in general terms. Beyond this, there are specific types of Apostles who function with greater emphasis in certain areas. We cannot attempt to put them all in the same "box," saying, "If you are an Apostle, then you must do _____." No, the functions of Apostles are as varied as the spheres of authority in God's Kingdom. When we see men and women functioning in the ways I have described so far, we cannot assume that they *are* Apostles, but we can know that they *may be* Apostles.

Spiritual Covering

One important aspect of a person's function and responsibility as an Apostle—and one that needs special emphasis and explanation here—is to provide spiritual covering (also called "apostolic covering"), which means to provide protection, prayer, counsel, and guidance to those who relate to us as Apostles. It also means shielding those people in times of spiritual warfare.

In the past, the word *covering* has stirred a lot of emotional reaction. There is both a positive and a negative meaning to the work *covering*. The negative meaning implies suppressing, limiting, holding down, and restricting. Thus when applied to "apostolic covering" to describe the responsibilities of an Apostle, the word was met with mixed emotions ranging from acceptance to anxiety, and everything in between. Most of the time, such resistance is the result of experiencing or hearing about a situation in which a so-called "Apostle" has used authority or position unwisely, or even hurtfully toward others. Though many such regretful instances have occurred, I urge us as believers to put aside negative connotations of the word *covering,* to let go of man-made interpretations of the term, and to return to the positive usage of the word.

The positive meaning of the word *covering* is to protect, to guard from attack, and provide security. Apostles should be building up ministries, never restricting or holding down people or taking advantage of them.

In recent times, many examples of proper apostolic covering have taken place in my ministry and in the ministries of others. Let me share two specific stories with you.

Apostles should be building up ministries, never restricting or holding down people or taking advantage of them.

A person was joining my network and coming under my apostolic covering. Simultaneously, it came to my attention this person was being "attacked" by another minister.

False accusations, gossip, back-biting, and such things were happening. As an Apostle, what was I to do?

As one who provided spiritual covering, I needed to get involved in the situation and talk to the parties involved. It was necessary for me to go in, hear them out, stop the problem, bring correction where needed, reach resolution, and clean up the mess. This intervention was necessary because if left unchecked, the situation could have done great damage to the ministers involved and to the body of Christ in that city.

Why was it important that I do the cleaning up? One, because the situation involved other people who were recognized as Apostles. Two, because one of the people was now under my covering and I had a responsibility to "protect" and guide that person, to literally "fight" for that person. Doing battle on behalf of others (which is an aspect of spiritual covering) requires someone who has the spiritual authority to deal with such matters at this level, namely an Apostle of peer level or higher (in other words, a greater level of experience) with those involved.

On another occasion, a distressed pastor in my sphere of authority called me to tell me that a woman he was counseling became angry when he told her she was out of order. She had stormed from the session shouting, "I will destroy you. I will tell people you molested me."

He called me and asked, "What do I do?"

Since I am his apostolic covering, I challenged him. "Did you touch her? Did you become suggestive in any way? Don't lie to me; tell me everything."

He declared none of these things had happened and that nothing he did or said could have been interpreted as suggestive. I knew this pastor, and I trusted him to tell me the truth because of our relationship. I told him, "If you do not tell me all the truth, I cannot protect you, I cannot fight for you." Again, he affirmed that nothing had happened.

My instructions to him were simple: "If that woman says anything and contacts you again, send her to me. I will handle her."

I immediately put my "covering," a shield, around him and told him to go home to his family and rest. I took on the battle on his behalf, and the matter was taken care of.

The spiritual war is intense in our time. Because invisible battles are raging in every area of society, the Church has great need of well-trained, experienced Apostles who are thoroughly equipped to carry out their responsibilities. One of the most important responsibilities of an Apostle is to serve as a strong, wise, godly spiritual source of spiritual covering.

> *...as we continue to receive and walk in revelation concerning Apostles and apostolic covering we will see the negative experiences of the past reversed and the blessings of true, godly spiritual covering released.*

What Covering Is *Not*

Before I close this chapter, I want to address a concern that almost always arises around the subject of spiritual or apostolic covering—the matter of "tithing to the Apostle." In the past, when the body of Christ was operating with "early revelation" about the restoration of the five-fold ministry, many Apostles or Prophets began to "ordain" (this was before the proper term, *commissioning,* which we now use, was accepted) people as Apostles and/or Prophets.

When this began to happen, it seemed to be assumed that

the person being ordained would "automatically" come under the covering of the person doing the ordaining.

Immediately, two things were to take place. One, the person being ordained was then under the covering of the Apostle who conducted the ordination, and two, he or she became a member of that person's network. This meant that the new Apostle or Prophet began to pay tithes to the Apostle who had ordained him or her.

The obvious advantage of this approach was that the more people an Apostle "ordained" the more money he or she received. This type of activity caused many pastors and leaders to "back off" from the apostolic movement because they saw it as nothing more than a "money-making machine." This impression has certainly hurt the restoration of the apostolic movement. But, as we continue to receive and walk in revelation concerning Apostles and apostolic covering we will see the negative experiences of the past reversed and the blessings of true, godly spiritual covering released.

CHAPTER 8

Apostles: People of Character

THOUGH APOSTLES DIFFER widely in function, calling, and spheres of authority, there is one overriding and indispensable characteristic that must be common to all: godly character. Even if a person has raised the dead, if he or she does not exhibit exemplary godly character, then credentials as an Apostle should be challenged. David Cannistraci aptly writes about this: "Signs, wonders and mighty deeds have their place to be sure, ... but having those graces and abilities in operation without the presence of character would be useless as well as harmful.... Apostleship is a matter of character above any other single quality" *(The Gift of Apostle: A Biblical Look at Apostleship and How God Is Using It to Bless His Church Today,* Ventura, CA: Regal Books, 1996).

The Outward Expression of the Inner Person

Character is the outward expression of who a person is on the inside. The character of a church leader includes: honesty, integrity, ministerial ethics, holiness, and being without malice and deceit. As spiritual leaders, Apostles must be blameless and above reproach (see 1 Timothy 3:2).

Does "blameless and above reproach" mean an Apostle is perfect? No. However, it should imply that a person has appropriated the power and victory of the Cross concern-

The character of a church leader includes: honesty, integrity, ministerial ethics, holiness, and being without malice and deceit.

ing all issues, strongholds, or situations the devil could take advantage of. When this is the case, the person will be living life in such a way that no one can point an accusing finger at him or her and get away with it. The past has been dealt with and forgiveness is evident because of the cleansing blood of Jesus.

Therefore, it is crucial that we place a premium on the character of a person before we officially recognize or commission him or her as an Apostle. Great confusion has arisen among churches and church leaders because peer-level Apostles have not taken time to evaluate the character of a leader before commissioning him or her as an Apostle.

Official recognition and commissioning of a person as an Apostle, when character is questionable, gives room for the devil and people to make accusations against that person, the leaders who commission that person, and the body of Christ in general.

Accountability

Apostles should have the highest level of accountability. According to James 3:1, those who teach will be judged more strictly than others. Peter Wagner calls this God's "double standard" of judgment. God seems to have one standard of judgment for His leaders and another for the rest of the Body of Christ. This would seem to imply an even stricter judgment for Apostles and Prophets, because they are called to lay the foundations of the Church and are often called not only to build, but also to bring correction.

For an Apostle to have the authority and credibility to bring correction to the churches or individuals, he or she must personally have an even higher level of character, credibility, and accountability in his or her own life.

Paul's Character, Credibility, and Authority

Spiritual credibility and authority are linked with character. The Apostle Paul was able to confront the Corinthian believers regarding their moral failures because he did not have any major unresolved issues in his own life. He could speak with great authority and integrity when he said to the believers in his sphere of influence: "Therefore I urge you to imitate me" (1 Corinthians 4:16), and "Follow my example, as I follow the example of Christ" (1 Corinthians 11:1). Apostles who cannot echo Paul's words *with integrity* to their followers should re-evaluate the validity of their apostolic call.

Character Sins and Spiritual Maturity

The Apostle Peter addresses the issue of character sins in his first epistle. In fact, he links character sins with spiritual immaturity when he writes: "Therefore, rid yourselves of all malice and all deceit, hypocrisy, envy, and slander of every kind. Like newborn babies, crave pure spiritual milk, so that by it you may grow up in your salvation" (1 Peter 2:1, 2).

Interestingly, we do not see in this verse any of the offenses we normally consider "big sins." We do not read of such offenses as murder, fornication, robbery, lying, or adultery. I believe that, in this verse, the Apostle Peter is stressing that all of those "bigger" issues should be dealt with when a person first accepts Christ as Lord and Savior. Then, as we walk with the Lord, we should be growing in our spiritual maturity, dealing with such matters as malice, "deceit, hypocrisy, envy, and slander of every kind."

> *...as we walk with the Lord, we should be growing in our spiritual maturity, dealing with such matters as malice, "deceit, hypocrisy, envy, and slander of every kind."*

Here Peter links the issue of a lack of spiritual maturity with the kind of character sins he mentions. Peter is making the point that God now wants to deal with a deeper area of the spirit, the area we call "character," in those who are growing up spiritually. We are not to remain "spiritual babies" forever; we are to "grow up" and become responsible believers in His Kingdom. We must become spiritually strong so we will have the strength to stand in the day of battle.

When we refer to a "character sin" or a "character flaw," we are not referring to occasional sins. However, when we refuse to take those occasional flaws of temper, manipulation, verbal abuse, or cheating to God and asking for His help in overcoming them so our hearts and behaviors will be changed, then those occasional sins can become character flaws because they have not been dealt with and have become habits or patterns that are evident in our everyday lifestyle.

A Key Issue for the Modern-Day Church

Today, as never before, the issue of spiritual maturity must be addressed in every local church.

For generations, churches have taken action when a person's life or behavior involved such egregious offenses as adultery, stealing church funds, or killing someone. Yet, we have long tolerated totally unacceptable behavior and ungodly conduct in the life of both believers and leaders.

The best way to correct this problem, hopefully before it happens, is to have an infrastructure through which we make disciples. Discipleship can be described as "character trans-formation." In this process, we shed our old life and take on more of the life and character of Jesus. For this reason, we have been given the mandate to "make disciples" (see Matthew 28:19) of all believers so they can be what God has designed them to be—a chosen people, a royal and holy priesthood who will declare His praises (see 1 Peter 2:9). God wants His Church to be a holy people whose exemplary lives and good works would cause even non-believers to praise God. He wants to raise a holy people who demon-strate spiritual maturity and excellent character so that our lives begin to show forth the praise and glory of God. That is also what the world wants to see.

However, too often in the Church we have put premiums on outward appearances, and we have prematurely appointed people with strong personalities or charisma to leadership positions. We must remember that character takes time to develop. We can accelerate biblical knowledge and even ministry skills, but *we can never rush character develop-ment.* Only time and pressure will reveal what is truly within a person—his or her character.

The Importance of Addressing Character Flaws

Remember, 1 Peter 2:1-3 reads, "Therefore, rid yourselves of all malice and all deceit, hypocrisy, envy, and slander of every kind. Like newborn babies, crave pure spiritual milk, so that by it you may grow up in your salvation, now that you have tasted that the Lord is good." In today's language, the Apostle Peter is saying bluntly, "Come on, Church. It's time to grow up." God wants to see spiritual maturity in His people.

Therefore, we need to watch out for those with character flaws, especially those with a spirit of ambition that seeks for power and position. The challenge arises in the development of a leader when he or she refuses to acknowledge his or her personal weaknesses and the need for change. Yet, often, such people are allowed to move into higher positions of leadership without correction in the important area of character.

In some cases, there is a need for the person to receive inner healing or deliverance for the deep-seated roots of personal weakness that may go back to childhood. In such instances, we must deal with each situation and each person individually. Sadly, these problems often grow worse because individuals refuse to allow God to work in their lives, and they refuse to seek help from other spiritual leaders or to allow others to correct and minister to them.

> *The challenge arises in the development of a leader when he or she refuses to acknowledge his or her personal weaknesses and the need for change.*

Be on the Look-Out

As we assess character, we also need to be watchful of a manipulative spirit. Those who have a manipulative spirit tend to use people for their own benefit and do not take responsibility for their decisions and actions. They often try to orchestrate situations in ways that make them look good in front of others. Thus when things go wrong, they do not take responsibility, and they often shift blame. This usually leads to abuse of individuals, especially verbal and emotional abuse. Sadly such people often seek for "titles" and recognition while lacking apostolic character and credibility.

The manipulative, controlling spirit has also been identified as a "Jezebel spirit." Anyone male or female, who manifests a Jezebel spirit, is also reflecting a spirit of witchcraft. This Jezebel spirit wants to cut off the Prophet and any prophetic voice. This spirit will come against godly leadership and try to control and manipulate until that leadership is destroyed and the purposes of God are set back.

Pride Out, Humility In

First Timothy 3:6 also warns us that one of the requirements for leadership is that a leader should "not [be] a novice, lest being puffed up with pride he fall into the same condemnation as the devil" (NKJV). Pride is indeed a deadly sin and can be one of the biggest obstacles to the apostolic ministry. However, Apostles are often misjudged on this point. This happens because people often see Apostles during times of ministry, when they are warring against spiritual forces. Under those circumstances, the Apostle may not demonstrate behavior that appears meek or humble to others because

Pride is indeed a deadly sin and can be one of the biggest obstacles to the apostolic ministry.

he or she is engaged in spiritual warfare, which demands a strong posture of spiritual authority that is usually evident to audiences or congregations. However, off the platform, at dinner, during times when they are not in that warring mode, you will discover that almost every true Apostle walks in humility that is quite evident.

Gordon Lindsay writes, "True Apostles will first manifest their apostolic ministry by humility" (Gordon Lindsay, *Apostles, Prophets, and Governments,* Dallas, TX: Christ for the Nations, Inc., 1988, p. 14). No one can be a true Apostle and not be humble. A true Apostle must be humble and not think that he or she is the only one who can hear from God or is always right. Humility must be a hallmark of every Apostle.

CHAPTER 9

The Basics of Commissioning

IN MY MINISTRY as an Apostle who travels extensively and interacts with many church leaders and members, more and more people want to know what it means to commission an Apostle and why commissioning is important.

Before I was commissioned as an Apostle, I saw no need to be commissioned. I did not want to be commissioned or think it would make any difference in my ministry. After all, I reasoned, I was certainly functioning as an Apostle in the church I pastored and was recognized as an Apostle in our nation of Singapore and in other nations where we were working. However, after much prayer and discussion with other contemporary Apostles, I decided to allow three highly-regarded Apostles to commission me.

After the commissioning, I continued to minister as I was accustomed to ministering, doing all the things I had always done. But several months later, I began to see and feel a difference in my ministry. Significant changes took place in three specific areas.

First, I experienced an increase in *revelation.* I began to see things in God's Word I had not seen before and to operate at a new level of spiritual understanding.

Second, I experienced an increase in *anointing*. I noticed myself functioning in a greater measure of grace, power, and divine enablement in my ministry than I had ever known before.

Third, I experienced an increase in *authority*. This certainly happened in the spiritual realm, as my spiritual authority increased. It also happened in terms of growth in the natural realm, as my sphere of authority on earth expanded.

My sphere of authority increased in nations where I had been ministering for years. I began to minister in new ways and at new levels. I noticed this personally, and other leaders confirmed it by commenting on the increase of revelation and spiritual authority that had become evident in my ministry.

> *...unless we recognize our Apostles and Prophets we will be missing two key anointings from the five offices that Jesus gave the Church.*

I have written extensively on this subject in my book *Commissioning,* but I also want to include some basic information on commissioning in this book because I believe it is a very important aspect of the contemporary apostolic ministry. It is also critical because unless we recognize our Apostles and Prophets we will be missing two key anointings from the five offices that Jesus gave the Church. These five offices where given to equip and build up the body of Christ so every believer could have the strength to stand.

Commissioning Explained

Simply stated, commissioning is the bringing forth of an alignment between heaven and earth. The act of commissioning brings forth an alignment on earth of God's choice and plan for this person to serve as an Apostle in His Kingdom, a plan that is already established in heaven.

Commissioning is an official recognition of the fact that God has called, equipped, and graced a person to serve in the five-fold ministry office of the Apostle, and it is a process unique to the office of the Apostle. This is because Apostles function in God's Kingdom as generals do in the military—at the highest level of authority. Therefore, the military term *commissioning* is used when they are set into office.

Commissioning is not the same as ordination, but should take place separate from and subsequent to ordination. Anyone called into the ministry can be ordained, but only Apostles are commissioned.

When the commissioning service takes place, it includes far more than a time of prayer and the laying on of hands. The act of commissioning releases power in the spiritual dimension. The commissioning service is a time to declare into the heavenlies that the person being commissioned is being released into a new level of authority in the earthly realm and in the spiritual realm. It is a moment of proclaiming to God that the new Apostle is formally acknowledged and received as a gift from Him to the Church.

> *Commissioning is an official recognition of the fact that God has called, equipped, and graced a person to serve in the five-fold ministry office of the Apostle....*

Being set in and commissioned as an Apostle does not indicate the beginning of a person's ministry; it provides official recognition of the fact that the person has already been ministering at the level of an Apostle for a period of time and has established a proven track record in ministry. Now, through commissioning, others affirm and accept what God has already been doing in and through that person's life and ministry.

Qualifications for Commissioning

Commissioning is a serious and solemn act that has ramifications both on earth and in the spiritual realm. Because it is so important to individuals being commissioned and to those who follow their leadership, it must not be done on a whim or without much prayer, thought, and planning. It also requires a process of assessing the personal lives and ministries of leaders who are candidates for commissioning.

First, let me clearly state that a person who takes it upon himself or herself to pursue commissioning as an Apostle is out of order. I will elaborate on this point later in this chapter, but for now let me simply state that the initiative for commissioning should never come from the leader himself or herself. The reason for this is that a person needs to be acknowledged first by those who know him or her. These people will have validated the candidate's ministry and affirmed his or her character, life, ministry, family, standards, and other important qualities. In other words, a candidate should not pursue commissioning unless and until others who recognize the person as an Apostle and believe that he or she is ready to be commissioned have already requested that commissioning take place.

As we consider those who may need to be commissioned in order to function in the full measure of authority in which God has designed for them to operate, we look for the following.

- those who function as Apostles.
- those who have the character of Apostles.

- those who have the mindset of Apostles.
- those whose ministries bear the fruit of an Apostle.

When these elements combine in a person's ministry and have been evident on a consistent basis over a period of years, there is a good chance he or she may be an Apostle.

In addition, firstly and most importantly, a candidate for commissioning must *know*, without any doubt or question, that *God* has called him or her into the office of an Apostle.

> *...a candidate should not pursue commissioning unless and until others who recognize the person as an Apostle and believe that he or she is ready to be commissioned have already requested that commissioning take place.*

Secondly, *the leaders* of the Apostle's local church or sphere of ministry need to affirm this person and agree that he or she is functioning as an Apostle, demonstrating the character that befits the office, and bearing the fruit of an Apostle's ministry.

Thirdly, *the congregation* of the Apostle's local church or ministry sphere also needs to affirm the person as an Apostle. This affirmation does not come by a voting process, but is evident as the people respond to the person and/or understand that he or she operates as an Apostle, walks in the character of an Apostle, and produces the fruit of an Apostle.

Fourthly, I do not believe that commissioning should take place unless there is an acceptable cross-section of the body of Christ who can affirm the person as an Apostle. Over the course of a ministry, an Apostle will have pioneered or helped establish other ministries and people who may not be part of his or her local church or sphere. These people need to attest to this person's ministry as an apostolic ministry—not just as a pastoral ministry, a prophetic ministry, or a teaching ministry, but really serving them as an Apostle. Even though these other components may also be present, the person must be leading the ministry primarily as an Apostle.

In addition, other people or groups may also affirm the person as an Apostle, which is certainly good and acceptable.

The Commissioning Process

Commissioning an Apostle should take place by an orderly and deliberate process that validates the Apostle's life and ministry. This process, which is explained in greater detail in my book *Commissioning,* should include the following:

1. Interview. If you are planning to commission someone as an Apostle, you will need to take time to interview the person. Provide an opportunity for the individual to talk with you about his or her call to ministry, readiness to step up to new levels of responsibility and authority, plus the general condition of his or her life and ministry. If the person is married, you also need to interview the spouse. Your goal in the interview process is to evaluate the person's life and character so that you can be certain it is order.

2. Ministry Review. Before a person is commissioned, his or her ministry needs to be examined carefully for tangible and verifiable proof of ministry impact. The key questions to ask are: "Does the candidate have a proven track record of ministry at the level of an Apostle?" and "Does he or she lead the ministry with humility and integrity, and according to biblical principles?"

3. Confirmation of Accountability. Before commissioning occurs, a candidate should be in an accountable relationship with one to three Apostles outside of his or her group. These Apostles will form the group who can remove the Apostle from ministry in the event of ethical, moral, or financial failure and can provide guidance or leadership in the restoration process if needed.

These relationships need to be reflected in writing and known by a larger group of peers.

4. Financial Review. Apostles often serve as stewards, trustees, or advisors in financial situations of the Kingdom, so their money matters should be reviewed and found above reproach before commissioning takes place.

5. Recommendations. Before commissioning, candidates should provide written recommendations from other people who know them well and understand the new levels of responsibility that will come with being commissioned. Candidates should expedite this process by giving the person in charge of commissioning the names and contact information of several individuals who will recommend them and instruct these people concerning where to send the completed recommendation forms.

The Commissioning Service

Because commissioning is the process by which Apostles are formally recognized and set into office, the commissioning service calls for formality, ceremony, dignity, and celebration.

The service should include music that is regal and worshipful. It is also an occasion to decorate a sanctuary or worship center with appropriate plants, greenery, flags, or items that reflect the dignity and stateliness of this ceremonial occasion. Those attending the service should wear their "Sunday best," which means suits for men and corresponding dress for women.

Participants in a commissioning service, in addition to the commissioning candidate, should include:

- **A master or mistress of ceremonies.** This person will open the service, welcome guests, make introductions, make any necessary announcements, present a review of the ministry of the candidate being commissioned, introduce people to give testimonies, lead in the offering, and perform other duties as needed or requested. If desired, more than one person can be selected to provide leadership in the different areas just mentioned.

- **The commissioning Apostle.** The candidate for commissioning should choose an Apostle of greater experience and authority to do his or her commissioning. This person will be the one to place the sword into the hands of the new Apostle and to release some of his or her authority into the new Apostle's life and ministry through the act of commissioning.

- **Members of the Apostolic Presbytery.** The Presbytery includes the commissioning Apostle, plus other Apostles and Prophets who will make apostolic-prophetic declarations over the candidate who is being commissioned as a new Apostle.

- **A Pastor.** Every believer, ministry leader, and five-fold minister needs a Pastor. While having a Pastor included in the commissioning service is not required, I believe it is a good idea because he or she will represent another of the five-fold offices.

- **A congregation or group of witnesses.** Commissioning should be a public event, an occasion to be shared with family, friends, ministry colleagues, and those who follow the person being commissioned as an Apostle.

The Order of Service

The order of service for a commissioning can vary from place to place and person to person. As a general guideline, I submit the outline below as a template that others have used and that you may wish to follow. In my book, *Commissioning,* you can find this information in greater detail and with photos.

1. Worship time. The music should be dignified and majestic, yet reverent and appropriate for a celebration as it ushers the congregation into true worship.

2. Welcome and introductions. The master or mistress of ceremonies should make everyone in attendance feel welcome to the service, introduce special guests, and convey to the audience a sense of the importance of the event.

3. Ministry review. The master or mistress of ceremonies recounts the history of the candidate's ministry and shares the "fruit" of his or her ministry.

4. Testimonies. The master or mistress of ceremonies introduces the board members (or equivalent) of the candidate's ministry. Any one of these people can share about the candidate and his or her fruit in ministry. If other people have also been chosen to share, they should do so at this time.

5. Offering. The master or mistress of ceremonies shares briefly from the Word, then receives the offerings, "seed offerings," and financial gifts. Music should be provided during this time.

6. Teaching on Apostles. The commissioning Apostle explains the ministry of Apostles. The teaching should also include a charge to the people and a charge to the Apostle being commissioned. This time of sharing leads into the commissioning time.

7. Presentation of Apostle and presbytery. The master or mistress of ceremonies calls forward by name the candidate being commissioned and those who form the apostolic presbytery. These people then come forward and take their positions. It is appropriate to play majestic music as the people are moving into place.

8. Anointing, Prayer, and Presbytery. The commissioning Apostle anoints the new Apostle. Then, the apostolic presbytery comprised of several Apostles and Prophets should release prayers, prophetic words, and apostolic-prophetic declarations over the new Apostle.

9. Commissioning. The commissioning Apostle then commissions the new Apostle. The actual commissioning is a high point and a solemn moment in the service. This includes additional exhortations, declarations, and the presentation of the sword by the commissioning Apostle to the new Apostle.

10. Apostolic-prophetic declarations. Additional apostolic and prophetic declarations should be released over the new Apostle. These declarations will be released into the heavenlies and recorded there. All should take notice of the recognition of God's gift (the new Apostle) to war against satan's kingdom.

11. Apostolic address. The new Apostle should address the congregation. This address need not be lengthy, but its tone should convey the strength and vision of the leader, while also being a true sharing of the Apostle's heart for the people and God's planned destiny for them.

12. Apostolic benediction. To close the service, the new Apostle should pronounce a benediction and dismiss the congregation.

Being commissioned as an Apostle truly is a significant event in a leader's life. Therefore, it is appropriate to send printed invitations to the ceremony and for those who receive invitations to give gifts to the person being commissioned. These gifts could include financial contributions or specific items for the new Apostle's ministry. Such gifts show honor to the new Apostle, sow seeds for increase into his or her ministry, and reflect the giver's heart of celebration.

CHAPTER 10

Transitioning into the Apostolic

ACCORDING TO DANIEL 2:21, 22, God Himself changes times and seasons. He is the one who sets kings and rulers in place in the nations of the earth, and He is the one who puts leaders into position in His Church. He knows that we will have different times and seasons in our lives as we grow and fulfill His plans for us, and He knows when the time is right for those seasons to change.

Perhaps, as you have been reading this book, you sense that God is changing times and seasons in your life and/or ministry. Maybe you sense that you need or want to transition into the apostolic as an individual—where your personal mindset is concerned—or as a leader who has influence and authority over a church or organization.

Personally, I have made several major ministry transitions over the years, including a transition into the apostolic. I have also led many churches and organizations through this process, including the church I pastored for almost thirty years, Trinity Christian Centre in Singapore. Through the years, I have noticed ten steps that are essential to successful transition into the apostolic, which I will share with you in this chapter.

A Season Change for Me

Before I focus on the steps of transition, I would like to relate a story about one of my first significant transitions in ministry. In the years before I became Pastor at Trinity Christian Centre, I had worked as a missionary and as a traveling Evangelist and was very happy in that ministry. I saw many salvations, miracles, and healings during that time, and conducted a number of successful meetings and crusades. Then, God spoke to me and let me know that I needed to become Pastor of a small church that had more problems than it had people. I had absolutely no desire to be a Pastor, but I knew God had spoken and I knew I needed to obey Him.

Making the transition from Evangelist to Pastor was not easy. It required me to change in more areas than I would have expected. For example, I was accustomed to traveling and speaking to different audiences on a regular basis—and I enjoyed that. But being a Pastor meant that I had to stay home and minister to the same people three times per week. As an Evangelist, I did not have to "dress up" except when I preached. But as a Pastor, I needed to wear business attire every day. This was quite an adjustment for me, as I much preferred blue jeans to "hose and heels." Furthermore, becoming a Pastor required me to approach my messages in new ways. I had to prepare them differently and to deliver them differently, because the purpose of an Evangelist's message is different than the purpose of a Pastor's message. As an Evangelist, I could have 5 sermons in my repertoire and preach them over and over again in dif-

> *Making the transition from Evangelist to Pastor was not easy. It required me to change in more areas than I would have expected.*

ferent places and to different audiences. But as a Pastor, I needed to serve "fresh bread" to the congregation each time we met. Believe me, this was a transition that I had to "work at" every day.

In more recent years, as I have left the full-time pastorate to serve as an Apostle, I have had to make other transitions. Thankfully, I now understand the process of transition better, which enables me to apply it in my own life and to help others as they move from one season in God to the next.

The Steps to Successful Transition

Successful transition into the apostolic does not happen quickly. In fact, it requires a deliberate plan, a strategic process, and enough time to lay firm foundations to build upon for years to come.

1. Make every level of leadership aware that transition is at hand. Help them all understand the process and intended result of the transition.

2. Expose leaders to apostolic and apostolic-prophetic teaching. Take them to conferences; give them relevant books to read or messages to listen to; and network them with others who are more experienced in the apostolic. Do whatever you can to help them learn.

3. Invite leaders who can speak to your church or organization about the apostolic. Allow your congregation to see these people flow in an apostolic-prophetic anointing. Let them experience this kind of ministry and become acquainted with Apostles and Prophets.

4. Identify yourself and your ministry at the appropriate time. There will come a time when you as a leader, and your ministry, can no longer continue to be "neither fish nor fowl." During transition, you will be in a time of discovery and you will be unable to "label" yourself or your ministry because your identity is still unfolding. However, over too long a period of time, failure to identify who you are and what you value will create confusion about your mission, purpose, and identity.

Begin to ask yourself, "What am I in ministry and what kind of organization am I going to lead?" Are you a Pastor? Are you an Apostle? Are you going to develop and lead an apostolic church? Or, are you going to take a pastoral approach? These are some of the important questions to be wrestled with during transition. Determine to identify yourself and your ministry, as I often say, "as soon as possible, but not prematurely."

5. If you are an Apostle, be commissioned—and do so properly and with excellence. If you are called and anointed to fulfill a five-fold ministry office, such as that of Apostle, allow yourself to be set into that office correctly, in such a way that you and others realize the importance and authority that accompanies your title. For more details on the process, protocol, and importance of commissioning, along with a step-by-step sample commissioning service with photos, please see my book *Commissioning.*

6. Be prepared for increased spiritual attack. Most of us have heard the phrase, "new level, new devil," and it is true. Every new level of authority, responsibility, or influence in God's Kingdom seems to also have an increased amount of intensity and/or frequency of spiritual warfare.

Read David's story in 2 Samuel 5:1-17. We see in this passage that, "When the Philistines heard that David had been anointed king over Israel, they went up *in full force* to search for him . . ." (2 Samuel 5:17, emphasis mine). The Philistines' offensive attack against David is surprising, especially since the time when Saul was angrily pursuing David, David had fled to Philistine territory because he knew he would be safe there. In fact, when thinking about the fact that Saul wanted to destroy him, David concluded, ". . . *the best thing I can do* is to escape to the land of the Philistines" (1 Samuel 27:1, emphasis mine).

According to 1 Samuel 27:7, David lived among the Philistines for more than a year, and we have no biblical information or indication that the Philistines tried to attack him during that time. Even though this took place after David had slain the Philistine giant, Goliath, we have every reason to believe that he lived peaceably among the Philistine people.

The interesting point here is that David had already been anointed king when he took refuge in the land of the Philistines. He had not yet ascended to the throne, but he had been set apart for the position. It was not until he actually became king, with all the authority and privileges of kingship, that the Philistines launched their attack against him.

There are different levels of authority in the kingdom of darkness, just as there are different levels of authority in God's Kingdom. Demonic forces are assigned to individuals, families, cities, and nations—and to every level of leadership. So, as you go through transition and find yourself with increased authority, influence, and responsibility, be aware that the spiritual warfare in your life is likely to intensify, so be ready to fight for new levels of victory.

7. Remember that transition is a process. Transition can be exciting. Especially if you are a visionary leader or one who adjusts to change easily, you may be tempted to want the process to move more quickly than it should. Changing a church or a ministry is a significant undertaking, one that should not be done too fast.

As you go through transition, keep in mind Deuteronomy 7:22: "And the Lord your God will drive out those nations before you little by little; you will be unable to destroy them at once, lest the beasts of the field become too numerous for you" (NKJV). This verse reminds us that the way to move forward wisely and make progress toward solid, lasting change is one step at a time, little by little. As a leader who is willing to cooperate with a long-term process of change, you will ensure that the greatest possible number of people understand and embrace the implications of the changes. This will help ensure that the changes take affect in every area where it is needed, and that the new mindsets and values associated with the change become firmly planted in your church or organization.

8. Identify other Apostles and Prophets as soon as possible, but not prematurely. Part of effective transition into the apostolic is to make sure that you are building other five-fold ministers. Especially where Apostles and Prophets are concerned, be watching for those under your leadership who may be emerging in these offices. Get them into leadership positions as soon as they are mature enough to handle the responsibilities.

9. Approach senior leadership change with a long-term perspective. In days gone by, Pastors commonly gave "three months' notice" when planning to retire or relocate to another place of service. This often left lay leaders within the church with the responsibility of finding a new Pastor. Many times, new Pastors did not build on the foundations the former Pastors had laid, and in effect, took churches "back to the drawing board" to come up with new direction, new mission, new values, and/or new culture for the church.

In an apostolic paradigm, every effort is made for one leader to lay foundations for the next and for new leaders to stand on the shoulders of former leaders. For this reason, I urge Pastors and Apostles who lead churches to begin identifying possible successors at least ten years before a successor will be needed, and to undertake a deliberate process of assessing leadership giftings and potential, character, preaching ability, administrative skills, etc. over that period of time.

I do not believe candidates should be aware that they are being considered as successors to the senior leader, but should be observed as they carry out their daily lives and responsibilities without knowing they are being assessed for future promotion. Let's face it: Everybody can be on their best behavior when they know someone is watching! As a leader, you want to see how they function "in the dark," so to speak, when they do not feel they are in the spotlight.

When six or seven years have passed, a senior leader should have a field of possible successors narrowed to one or two (preferably one) and should begin the intentional process of grooming that leader for the senior position.

10. Build a safety net. All ministry leaders need to be accountable to someone. In the case of Apostles, every Apostle should have a covering, or a relationship with one-to-three other Apostles who have the authority to remove the Apostle from leadership in the event of heresy, moral failure, financial impropriety, or other grievous offenses.

As you can see, transitioning into the apostolic takes time, effort, and strategy. But having worked with many churches, ministries and leaders who have made this transition, I can assure you that the benefits outweigh all the time and energy required to make the shift.

You may be asking, "Why is transitioning into the apostolic so important?" The answer lies at the root of this book. The Church at large seems to have shifted from laying strong biblical foundations in people's lives to more of an entertainment, "get the crowds in" approach to ministry. In many cases, the philosophy has become, "Get them in, stroke them, and boost them up enough to get them through another seven days until they can return for another 'booster' shot for another week."

Of course there are exceptions to my observation, but I am addressing a major "felt need" in the body of Christ. We desperately need to train and equip all believers, so they can not only have the strength to stand but also have the spiritual preparation to function in their God-given anointings and ministries. These expressions of ministry may be in the local church, or in the marketplace.

The challenge we have faced in the past and continue to face today is *how* to grow and develop people who have the strength to stand. The Bible tells us that everything that can be shaken will be shaken. Then we must ask ourselves how we develop unshakable believers who dare to declare that they can change the world for Jesus.

Section III:

The Prophetic Ministry

CHAPTER 11

The Purpose and Importance of the Prophetic Ministry

FOR THE CHURCH to develop the strength needed to stand in our day and in the days to come, it must have an apostolic-prophetic foundation. I remind you that Apostles and Prophets lay the foundations of the Church (see Ephesians 2:20), and we need Apostles and Prophets to work together for the foundations to be firm and stable.

Throughout the body of Christ, there are many impressions and schools of thought concerning the definition, purpose, and importance of the prophetic ministry. In this chapter, I will address these three aspects of the prophetic because clear understanding is needed in order to establish a prophetic ministry that functions properly and contributes rightly to the life, strength, and growth of local churches and the Church as a whole.

Understanding the Prophetic Ministry

Prophetic ministry is one aspect of the Holy Spirit's ministry in the lives of believers today. On the simplest and most basic level, prophecy is God's speaking through a man or woman. Prophetic ministry takes place when Holy Spirit anoints a believer with supernatural abilities to perceive, show, demonstrate, or articulate the words, desires, ways, goals, or passion of God. The Holy Spirit works and moves through each of us and anoints us with a special ability to perceive and express God's heart to others through spoken or written words, music, or other forms of expression. The prophetic ministry comes through believers, but it originates in the heart of God.

Prophetic ministry takes place when Holy Spirit anoints a believer with supernatural abilities to perceive, show, demonstrate, or articulate the words, desires, ways, goals, or passion of God.

In Acts 2:1-4 and 17-21, we read that the Holy Spirit came to earth on the Day of Pentecost. In verse 17, we see that the Holy Spirit is poured out on *all* people. As a result, all those who have received the Holy Spirit can move in prophecy; the gift of prophecy is available to us, and we can know and express what God is saying and doing.

The word *prophecy* comes from the Greek word *propheteia,* which means "to forthtell, to predict, speak under an inspiration or to be able to foretell." God is always speaking, and in prophecy, He uses us to speak forth or communicate His message. Prophecy also includes foretelling, which means we are able to predict or speak forth the things God shows us will happen in the future.

Much of the prophecy we read in the Bible is both foretelling and forthtelling—the foretelling of the events that God orchestrates and brings in the future, as well as the forthtelling of God's heart to His people.

Types of Prophecy

In the Old Testament, we generally see two types of prophecy, represented by two different words. The first is *naba,* which connotes the idea of a bubbling forth or a bursting forth and it gives us the idea of the word of God coming forth spontaneously. It is almost like an explosion and a spontaneous flow or release. The second word is *nataf,* which carries the idea of falling like rain or dropping like dew. This concept of prophecy is softer and gentler, like the falling of God's word on our hearts. In both cases, prophecy means a "now" word, a current message that is a gift of God and comes to human hearts for a specific purpose.

In the New Testament, we also see two words for prophecy: *logos,* which is the written Word of God, and *rhema,* which is a spoken word to accomplish God's purposes for a specific time. The *rhema* word will never contradict the *logos* (written) Word. As we move in prophecy, a prophetic word should never contradict the Scriptures. The Bible has already given us principles and standards for life, and no prophetic word should contradict it.

To be effective and flow powerfully in the prophetic gift, we must have a good understanding of the heart and mind of God as revealed through His Word. We have a responsibility to grow in the *logos* Word so we can minister His *rhema,* "now" word on the foundation of His truth expressed in Scripture.

> *To be effective and flow powerfully in the prophetic gift, we must have a good understanding of the heart and mind of God as revealed through His Word.*

Purposes of Prophecy

The prophetic ministry is for groups of believers who are assembled together and for individuals. Its three main purposes are:

- to edify (to build, to strengthen, and to make more effective)
- to exhort (to stimulate, to encourage, and to admonish)
- to comfort (to cheer up)

Because the primary purposes of the gift of prophecy are to edify, to exhort, and to encourage, the prophetic ministry can help people overcome two of satan's most common attacks: condemnation and discouragement.

Condemnation renders us weak and ineffective because it keeps us focused on our pasts and prevents us from moving forward. Because of the sins and mistakes of our pasts, many of us need to be set free, and prophecy can help us break free because it strengthens us, encourages us, and cheers us up.

Prophecy also breaks the power of discouragement in our lives. When believers are discouraged, churches are ineffective because we lose our sense of purpose and power. We feel we are not making a difference or being productive in our lives, no matter how hard we try. The gift of prophecy can overcome the enemy's work of discouragement and release us into the freedom and joy of pursuing our purpose in God.

Prophecy builds up and strengthens individuals and churches to become all God wants us to be and to do everything He wants us to do.

When condemnation and discouragement are kept out of the hearts of believers and out of churches, strength and power arise, and God's people become effective in His service. Prophecy builds up and strengthens individuals and churches to become all God wants us to be and to do everything He wants us to do.

The Importance of the Prophetic Ministry

As believers who are full of the power of the Holy Spirit, the prophetic ministry flows through us into everything we do and impacts every dimension of our lives and ministries. It is important in the lives of individual believers and in the corporate life of local churches and the Church universal for five primary reasons.

1. The prophetic ministry brings a greater level of intimacy and strength into our relationship with God. One of the most basic and profound expressions of the prophetic ministry is bringing people back to their first love. If we look at all the prophetic books in the Bible, one of the simplest messages from the prophets was a call to the nations of Israel and Judah to return to God, their first love—to repent of their sins and turn from their wicked ways. This is still one of the most important messages of the prophetic ministry because God is always calling people back to Himself. He continually wants to restore the relationship between mankind and Himself.

One of the anointings on the prophetic ministry is to be able to communicate the love of God to people and to bring them to a place of responding to that love. Many, many people today need breakthroughs in their understanding of

God's love for them. Many also need to understand that they are prostituting themselves and staying distant from God by virtue of the way they live their lives, and they need to know God wants their hearts to return to Him. The prophetic voice of the Lord calls people back to a place of intimacy and strength in Him. Often, Prophets and those who move in the prophetic ministry are able to present the Word of God and the person of Jesus in a way that empowers people to receive the call of God in their lives again.

2. The prophetic ministry increases our maturity. According to Ephesians 4:11, 12, God gave the five-fold ministry to the Church for the purpose of building people, the body of Christ, to maturity in Christ. The role of the Prophet is to work together with the Apostle and the other five-fold offices to accomplish this. The gifts of Apostle and Prophet are both necessary if we want to see the body of Christ come to maturity; and these gifts must operate in fullness. God's

One of the anointings on the prophetic ministry is to be able to communicate the love of God to people and to bring them to a place of responding to that love.

plan is for all five to work together. So, they function as a team to equip the saints and to raise the church to a place of maturity. Specifically, Prophets receive revelation, and they perceive and release the word of the Lord into situations and into people's lives; and Apostles help strategize and accomplish the fulfillment of these words.

3. The prophetic ministry releases the gifts of the Holy Spirit and ministry callings. Many gifts are released through prophecy and the laying on of hands. In 1 Timothy

1:18 and 4:14, Paul encouraged Timothy to remember the gifts imparted to him through the laying on of hands and the prophetic ministry, and reminded him to continue to fan into flames the gifts he received.

The prophetic ministry releases the anointing of God and the revelation of the gifts He has given to the body of Christ so His people can live with a sense of purpose in our hearts. This way, we will know what God has desired and called us to do, and we can step into that anointing. Not only does a release of the revelation of God take place through the prophetic ministry, this ministry also releases a flow of God's anointing. When a prophetic word is released and people receive prophetic ministry, a powerful impartation occurs. Through the gift of prophecy, we receive the impartation of the Holy Spirit and an anointing that raises us to a new place in God.

4. The prophetic ministry brings greater revelation of the end-time purposes of God. We are living in the last days. Signs of the times are happening around us in increasing measure. We do not have as much time to fulfill God's purposes as generations before us have had. Everywhere we look, we see evidence of the world's desperation and the increase of evil. At the same time, God is pouring out a prophetic anointing on the Church so we will have an understanding of His purposes in this hour and be gripped with a sense of urgency to fulfill those purposes.

The prophetic ministry helps us discern what God is saying, what He is doing, and how He is directing us to use our time and resources to fulfill His desires and accomplish His purposes. We have limited time and resources, so it is crucial that we seek the Lord and make sure that we are investing in

His purpose for this hour. We are accountable to God for the resources He puts in our hands, and the prophetic ministry can help us know how to use them.

5. The prophetic ministry brings strength and edification to the Church. As you have read already, one of the most basic purposes of the prophetic ministry is to bring strength and edification to the body of Christ (see 1 Corinthians 14:3). As leaders, we want to see the body of Christ step out in faith and begin to do the works of God. In reality, as we minister to them, we are often caught up in dealing with the problems they face, and we find ourselves challenged as we try to help them move forward into the purposes of God. One of the great things about the prophetic ministry is that it makes possible a breaking through of the Spirit of God to bring strength and edification so that people are no longer focused on their problems. Through the prophetic ministry, God helps them see from His perspective. One of the purposes of the gift of prophecy is to build up both the Church as a whole and believers as individuals. It gives them strength and hope, turns their focus away from themselves and their problems and onto the greatness of God, and helps them do what He wants them to do.

CHAPTER 12

Prophets in the Church Today

FOR THE MODERN-DAY Church to gain strength to stand, we must understand the ministries of both Apostles and Prophets. Just as many people who function apostolically or demonstrate apostolic mindsets and abilities are often erroneously referred to as Apostles, many prophetic people are often called Prophets. Most of the time, this happens innocently and only because the Church has not had a full understanding of what a Prophet is and what Prophets do in the body of Christ. But, when such titles are used prematurely or wrongly, confusion and frustration often result.

Just as all believers are apostolic in the sense that they called to live with a knowing that they are "sent" by God, all believers should also be prophetic in the sense that they can hear God's voice. But, all believers do not necessarily operate in the gift of prophecy, and all believers do not have a five-fold ministry call to the office of the Prophet. In this chapter, I want to clearly explain how we identify Prophets, how they function, and the various types of Prophets in the Church today.

The Office of the Prophet

Ephesians 4:11 specifically mentions Prophets as one of God's five-fold ministry offices. Functioning in the office of the Prophet is much different than moving in the gift of prophecy. When we use the word *Prophet,* we are referring to a person God has called into the office of the Prophet, not someone who moves in the gift of prophecy.

The office of the Prophet is an appointment of God, not an appointment of man. In other words, a person cannot decide one day to declare himself or herself a Prophet. God appoints those He chooses and desires to serve Him as Prophets. *The recognition of man will accompany the appointment of God.* When God appoints a Prophet, people will recognize God's appointment and the ministry in that person's life. Now, this is an important truth because we often switch the order.

> *The office of the Prophet is an appointment of God, not an appointment of man.*

Prophetic people see or sense an "appointment" by man, and then hope desperately for recognition from God. It doesn't work that way. When God calls a Prophet, He appoints that person. When God appoints Prophets, He designs what He wants them to do and how He wants them to function. Prophets have a very clear sense of the destiny and mission of God in their lives.

The office of the Prophet has authority invested in it. This authority enables Prophets to function in a realm of authority higher than the realm in which those with the gift of prophecy function. One of the recognizable dynamics about a person in the office of the Prophet is that God invests spiritual authority into that person to be able to fulfill what He desires.

Recognizing a Prophet

We know that Prophets and the prophetic ministry provide valuable gifts to the Church today, but we also need to know how to distinguish between those who operate in the gift of prophecy and those whom God has called to serve in the office of the Prophet. When trying to identify a true Prophet or someone who is moving into the office of the Prophet, look for these signs.

1.   A witness in the heart of the Prophet. Everyone who functions in a five-fold ministry office must first be called and appointed by God. True Prophets have an unshakable witness in their hearts of this divine call. These individuals *know*—with a deep knowing in their spirits—that they are called and appointed by the Lord to serve Him and His people as Prophets. In addition to this heartfelt confidence, Prophets will also sense that God is training them to serve in this office.

2.   Recognition from other Prophets. This is important, because people recognize others who share their calling and anointing. If God has called a person to be a Prophet, it will be evident to other Prophets. They will recognize the gift and the call, the ministry and office in which Prophets function.

3.   Recognition from spiritual leadership. When God calls a Prophet in the Church today, He aligns him or her with other five-fold leaders to serve and minister in the body of Christ. Spiritual leaders should recognize and affirm that God has set Prophets in that place.

4. Recognition from the body of Christ. Those who are in close relationships with the Prophet will recognize that person as a Prophet. These people will see the ministry and office of the Prophet flowing in every dimension of the person's life.

5. Evidence of the prophetic ministry. When we look for evidence of the prophetic ministry in the life of a Prophet, we look for the "three A's," which are: anointing, accuracy, and authority. The prophetic ministry is evident in the high level of accuracy of words and revelation the Prophet receives. There will also be a tremendous anointing on the words to accomplish what the purposes for which they are released, and the authority of God will be evident in the Prophet's life and ministry.

6. Character. Character is really the first mark of a true Prophet, and it is the "fruit" of a Prophet's life. Many times, we think the mark of a true prophet is the prophetic gifting, but the gifting actually ranks least in the signs of recognition. A prophetic gift is easy for God to release in a person, but character is what He wants and develops in the personal life and ministry of a true Prophet.

7. The prophetic spirit. The prophetic spirit is the second mark of a Prophet. The prophetic spirit speaks of the anointing, of the authority that the prophet carries, and of a spirit that is keenly in tune with and sensitive in God. This sensitivity to God, the things of God, and the spiritual realm releases Prophets to function in the anointing and authority of God in their lives.

8. The ability to bear the Lord's burden. The third mark of a Prophet is the ability to bear the burden of the Lord. When Jesus was on the cross, He bore our sins once and for all. We do not bear the sins of the world anymore, but we do bear the burdens of the Lord's heart. The ability to perceive and bear these spiritual burdens is evident in the life of a Prophet. Prophets are often burdened by the very burden of the things of God. This is why Prophets often carry a burden for the lost or such a burden for a particular church or a particular nation. The Lord is the One who places those burdens, and in so doing, He is sharing His heart with the Prophet.

According to Amos 3:7, God reveals His secrets to His Prophets. God shares the deep things, the secrets, and the burdens of His heart with His Prophets. He wants to know if a Prophet is able to carry His secrets, His burdens. When that happens, the Prophet will pray, intercede, and war with the burden; that is part of the call of the Prophet.

Many times when a Prophet begins to hear the secrets of the Lord, they will be a burden upon that person's heart because he or she recognizes the weight of the revelation and knows he or she has been counted worthy to stand together with Him and to bear those burdens. Just as the heart of a Prophet will be broken by the things that break the heart of God, it will also rejoice in the things in which God's heart rejoices.

Types of Prophets Today

Four primary types of Prophets are functioning in the Church today. These Prophets function according to their spheres of authority.

1. Local church Prophets. The sphere of authority of a local church Prophet is limited to the local church. These Prophets function in submission to the local church Pastor, and they are responsible for the prophetic ministry in their local church.

2. Regional Prophets. Simply put, the sphere of influence of a regional Prophet covers a certain region, meaning that it extends beyond the local church to a city, a nation or nations, or a group of churches. Regional Prophets must function in submission to an Apostle. They are responsible to work together with an Apostle for the breakthrough of God in those regions and to release God's word to that region. Sometimes, local church Prophets grow to become regional Prophets as God leads them. To avoid misunderstandings and disunity when this happens, some kind of relationship should be in place between the Apostle and the local church Pastor to whom the Prophet submits.

3. Presbytery Prophets. Their influence of presbytery Prophets is generally in the realm of giving prophetic words. They may function as individuals or as teams, and they may by localized or mobile. Whatever the case, these Prophets strengthen and build up the body of Christ by releasing personal prophetic words in people's lives.

4. Revelatory Prophets. The revelatory Prophets' sphere of ministry is limited to their revelation. They function by seeking the Lord for revelation and responding accordingly. Those who are revelatory Prophets today are usually set in positions where they can wait and hear from God. They are then responsible to respond to what they hear, whether it is praying and interceding only or by delivering the word to the appropriate person or people who need to act on it. An example is John the revelator, who wrote Revelation.

CHAPTER 13

Roles and Functions of Modern-Day Prophets

IN THE OLD TESTAMENT, Prophets functioned as emissaries of God who had sole and final authority. In the New Testament, Prophets function differently and do not have such ultimate authority. In the Church today, they function in a variety of ways and fulfill a number of roles. All of their roles and functions are important, but the important key to a Prophet's ministry today is to function in submission to and in unity with Apostles, Pastors, and the other five-fold gifts. The New Testament model of prophetic ministry is one of a team, and this is vital to remember as we consider the prophetic ministry today. This team approach is healthy for those who serve as Prophets and for the body of Christ.

A number of the important roles Prophets fulfill and functions they serve are listed below. This list is comprehensive but not exhaustive. In other words, the absence of a specific role or function from this list does not mean a Prophet cannot fulfill it.

Roles and Functions

1. Giving prophetic words. One reason God calls Prophets and sets them in the body of Christ is to give prophetic words—to edify, exhort, and encourage His people. These words may be personal, corporate, national, or international. Now, those who move in the gift of prophecy have also been called to give personal words and a valid ministry takes place when they give those words.

First Corinthians 14:3 teaches us that those who give words of prophecy do so to encourage, edify, and comfort the body of Christ. Those in the office of the Prophet can certainly give prophetic words in the realm of edification, exhortation, and comfort, but they also give words that go beyond those purposes because Prophets have both the anointing and authority of God to provide direction—to hear what God is saying and to bring His revelation to the body of Christ in the form of direction.

In the Old Testament, we see this often, when kings ask Prophets for direction in certain matters. In the New Testament, God also uses Prophets to bring direction, but they do so in submission to authority in leadership and with a spirit of unity toward the body of Christ.

Prophets can give prophetic words of direction and rebuke. For example, God called the Prophet Nathan to rebuke David and give him an authoritative word of correction and judgment. In the New Testament, Prophets can also carry words of correction, rebuke, or judgment—but they do not do so as the sole authority in a matter. They function together with the leadership to build up the body of Christ.

When Prophets give prophetic words in the way just described, something more than the gift of prophecy is in action. Because of the authority and mantle of the Prophet, such words are prophetic declarations. These words carry a stronger authority than words released through the gift of prophecy. This is not to minimize the gift of prophecy; it is powerful and necessary in the body of Christ. Words released from the office of the Prophet, however, have the authority and the anointing to change and shift atmospheres to facilitate and enable what God wants to do.

2. Prophetic pronouncement. A prophetic pronouncement is slightly different than a prophetic word. Most of the time, prophetic words are "conditional prophecy." They are conditional on the recipient's receiving them. A prophetic pronouncement is different in that it is not conditional. It is a pronouncement of the will of God; it can be a blessing or a judgment; and it is released when the Prophet has heard from the Lord what He will do. With a pronouncement, the result is "yea and amen."

In 1 Samuel, we read that the Lord used Samuel powerfully in the area of prophetic pronouncements. He pronounced Saul as king; he pronounced David as king; and he pronounced judgment on Saul when he disobeyed the Lord. Saul was utterly powerless to revoke the judgment. Even when he grabbed Samuel and ripped off the edge of his cloak, begging for mercy, the judgment could not be canceled.

Prophets today can be used to release prophetic pronouncements, and prophetic pronouncements are powerful. Prophets must be careful in this area of ministry and be sure to walk in submission to the leadership of the body of Christ.

3. Anointing ministries. In the Old Testament, God used Prophets to anoint ministries. The first king, Saul, was anointed by the Prophet Samuel. In the New Testament, this ministry carries on in a slightly different manner. God uses Prophets to release anointing and blessing on ministries, businesses, families, offices, marriages, etc.

4. Cleansing. One of the major roles of the Prophets today is to bring cleansing into the house of God. This is done by dealing with unrighteousness, ungodliness, and sin. The Prophet is uniquely anointed by God to deal with sin and to deal with it powerfully, in very focused ways.

Though all believers as individuals and all church leaders should deal with sin, God specifically anoints and appoints Prophets to be involved in the cleansing of the house of God, to raise the standards of purity and holiness.

The Church must be a pure and holy bride for Jesus Christ. This is why God wants to bring holiness and greater levels of intimacy into His people. Prophets call the body of Christ to return to their first love again and to increased intimacy with God. Those who move in the gift of prophecy can encourage people to return to their first love or deal with sin in their lives, but the Prophet's function is to bring cleansing both into individuals and into the corporate body. In a world of compromise, prophets will bring a clear sense of cleansing.

5. Serving as watchmen. One of the roles of Prophets is to be watchmen, to deliver warnings before a tragedy or an impending attack. They are involved in the protection of the body of Christ and of defending the body (keeping the enemy out). Prophets in the body of Christ today are called to function as watchmen so they can discern the attacks of the enemy, discern strategies for victory over the enemy, sound the trumpet call for the body of Christ to arise, and pray for protection and the ability overcome the attacks of the enemy.

Prophetic intercessors can also function in these ways, and they are also called by God as watchmen. But the Prophet's role is to lead the prophetic intercessors, judge their revelations, and empower them to grow in their prophetic giftings so the walls of defense in the body of Christ continue to stand high, and the works of the enemy can be overcome.

6. Warring. God calls Prophets to be warriors in the body of Christ. He anoints Prophets with warring spirits so they can lead in spiritual battles. They do this by functioning as spiritual intelligence agents, discerning divine strategies to overcome and to fulfill the purposes of God.

The body of Christ is advancing, and should be breaking through the gates of hell. The Church should be growing and conquering. One of the sad realities of many churches today is that they are inward focused, and they spend much time defending, guarding, and protecting what they have. This is why we have watchmen.

But churches also need to advance. Prophets work together with Apostles and Pastors to mobilize the body of Christ to accomplish this purpose and move churches forward to advance God's kingdom. Prophets also lead the prophetic intercessors into battle and discern and judge the revelations the prophetic intercessors receive.

7. Laying foundations. God calls Prophets today to lay foundations in the Church (see Ephesians 2:20); Prophets are involved in building and laying foundations for the body of Christ. In Ephesians 4:12, 13, we read that Prophets are to be involved in preparing God's people for the works of ministry—to build the people in faith and knowledge, to bring them to maturity, and to help them attain the fullness of Christ. Prophets and Apostles work together to build the local church and body of Christ, to give it strength to stand and fulfill the purposes of God.

8. Prophetic presbytery. A prophetic presbytery can serve as a venue for the impartation of spiritual gifts, for setting apart of prophetic ministries, and for ministering to leaders. On any prophetic presbytery team, it is important to have at least one person who is called to the office of the Prophet.

9. Mentoring. The prophetic mantle is passed on through mentoring relationships. For this reason, Prophets are involved in identifying and training emerging Prophets. Certainly, God can take someone and train him or her as a Prophet without human help. The forerunners of the prophetic ministry did not have mentors in their lives, but they made many mistakes, and the process was long. Modern-day Prophets who function as mentoring Prophets can train and equip emerging Prophets; they can help them avoid mistakes and expedite the process of seeing them commissioned and released as Prophets.

10. Healing ministries. Jesus has empowered the Church to move in signs, wonders, and miracles. Anyone in the body of Christ can move in healing, but Prophets have a unique call of God in the body of Christ to champion the healing ministries, simply because they are much more open to the spiritual realm in their lives and ministries.

Faith is a key dynamic in the internal makeup of the Prophet, Because of this, Prophets are able to encourage, support, move in, and bring about the miraculous move of God in their personal lives, and to empower others to see it happen in their lives too.

11. Setting up prophetic schools. Prophets are involved in the administration of prophetic schools and ministries in the body of Christ, and serve on the faculties of these training schools. This is another way they train and mentor emerging Prophets and others in the body of Christ.

12. Receiving revelation. Every believer has the privilege of receiving revelation from God, but Prophets tend to hear continuously through dreams, visions, and divine revelation. They then bring the revelation they receive to the body of Christ. Many times when God begins to call a Prophet, there will be an awakening of the prophetic spirit, which will be evident by an increase in the revelation that person receives.

13. Judging revelation. Because of the ability to receive revelation, and their experience and expertise in the prophetic language and terminology, Prophets can help emerging Prophets and those with the prophetic spirit to judge and discern the revelation they receive. Prophets bear witness to the revelation of God that comes from the body of Christ and are involved in the interpreting of dreams and visions. They also help mentor others in this process.

14. Confirmation. New Testament Prophets function strongly in the area of confirmation. In the Old Testament,

God spoke to certain people, but in the New Testament, He speaks to all believers. One of the roles of a Prophet is to confirm what God is speaking. Where the leadership of the Church is concerned, God often speaks to those in five-fold ministry offices and then uses Prophets to release confirmation of His word.

CHAPTER 14

Becoming a Prophetic Church and Establishing Prophetic Ministry in the Local Church

A CHURCH THAT HAS strength to stand in the intensity of our times will be a strongly prophetic church. It cannot simply be a church with "good prophetic ministry," but it needs to be a prophetic church.

What is a Prophetic Church?

Simply stated, a prophetic church is a church that is released to hear the word of God. This means every expression of ministry in the church has the dimension of hearing God's voice. For example, in a prophetic church, listening for His voice is incorporated into the leaders' meetings. When they plan, they think not only in terms of programs and systems, they also place great value on seeking God and hearing what He says. Another example concerns worship. A prophetic church not only sings prophetic songs, but members are taught to sing back to God what He is saying to their hearts.

The Book of Jeremiah talks about the song of the bride and the song of the bridegroom.

A prophetic church also receives the ministry of the Apostle and the Prophet. It is very dangerous to be prophetic and apostolic without the ministry of the Apostle and the Prophet inside the church. A church can have wonderful prophetic worship, but if there is no apostolic alignment and no apostolic direction and principle given, emotionalism and all sorts of complexities can result. Again, a prophetic church not only hears God's voice, but His word is integrated into every ministry of the organization and every level of leadership.

A prophetic church does not happen accidentally; it emerges deliberately. It must be thought through and well planned. It must also be administrated in four primary ways.

Administrate the Prophetic

Worship is a good example of the need to administrate the prophetic. Worship with no prophetic element is not good. But, neither is it good for worship leaders to be unprepared and simply spend 45 minutes singing in tongues. That can be detrimental to churches. The same is true in other areas of ministry. The prophetic dimension is important, but it must be executed sensitively, wisely, and with order.

A prophetic church does not happen accidentally; it emerges deliberately.

Administrate Prophecy

The way to administrate prophecy is to establish prophetic protocol. This will be explained in detail in the next chapter.

Administrate the Prophets

The nature of prophetic ministry is very charismatic and very spontaneous, and some Prophets confuse spontaneous word and spontaneous behavior. If a Prophet behaves spontaneously on a regular basis, the church will have problems. Administrating Prophets often begins with simple teaching on basic rules of relationship, engagement, and behavior, and continues with consistent enforcement of protocol.

Administrate the Ministry of the Prophet's Relationship with the Other Five-fold Gifts

A church with strength to stand is not a church where Apostles and Prophets feel celebrated while Pastors, Teachers, and Evangelists feel marginalized. Think, for example, about a meeting involving a Pastor and a Prophet. Prophets are often gifted verbally and can seem quite strong. If such a Prophet attends a planning meeting, and uses strong words, such as, "God spoke to me and said we should do this," then a Pastor may not feel comfortable questioning the Prophet. The pastoral ministry, by nature, seldom uses words like this. If Prophets are not administrated properly, Pastors and other leaders on the team will begin to feel unappreciated and unimportant. Encourage Prophets to express themselves prophetically but to also learn to be mature enough to use language that is inclusive. No one wants to contradict a Prophet who says, "God said . . ." We must work as teams in ministry and allow each member of the team to bring the best out of their giftings.

A prophetic church is strong, vibrant, and visionary. It is a church on the move, but it must be led well.

Establishing a Prophetic Ministry in a Local Church

Here are seven steps to establishing a prophetic ministry in a local church.

1. The Pastor must decide what he or she wants in the church. The worst possible reason to become an apostolic-prophetic church is that another church has become an apostolic-prophetic church. The decision to become apostolic-prophetic must be based on the leading of God's Spirit and on the conviction that apostolic-prophetic foundations enable the building of strong, vibrant, healthy churches. If the Pastor desires an apostolic-prophetic church, he or she must take responsibility for leading the church through the transition into the apostolic-prophetic.

2. The Pastor must take the lead, or at least lead the process. Most Pastors love their churches, but the nature of the pastoral ministry is very protective. Pastors are shepherds and sometimes make changes only after much prayer and careful consideration, and with great caution. If a Pastor wants a prophetic ministry in the church, he or she should take lead in establishing the ministry or appoint a trustworthy person who works well with the Pastor to lead the process, while the Pastor maintains a high level of oversight.

3. Determine the philosophy of your prophetic ministry. A philosophy is an expression of the ministry. How do you determine the philosophy of your prophetic ministry? Understand the philosophy of your church. For example, some churches are quite structured. They value discipline and strong, focused leadership. As a result of that, the way prophecy is expressed in those churches is also quite structured, with much protocol and with structured training for people who minister prophetically.

4. Set prophetic protocol. Prophetic protocol will be addressed in detail the next chapter, but know now that it is important to define the policies and procedures for prophetic ministry. This protocol should be clearly communicated to all appropriate people and enforced on a consistent basis. This provides safety and protection for those who minister prophetically, those who receive prophetic ministry, and those who observe the prophetic ministry. Prophetic protocol should reflect the church or ministry to which it applies and should be adapted as the organization grows and matures.

5. Develop a curriculum. A curriculum can be developed using existing books and prophetic curricula. Take ideas and material from a variety of sources. Be sure to include teaching in these areas: spiritual life and development, letting the Spirit of God impact you and move in your life; hearing God's voice; growing in the prophetic; and the Prophet in relation to other five-fold ministries.

6. Build your prophetic core. Don't attempt start a prophetic ministry by setting up a large conference, but begin with a small core group of people. The first group should be men and women who love the prophetic. Also, develop it among the church staff, but not in a covert or hidden way.

7. Stir up the gifts among the Pastors, leaders, and congregation. The stirring of the gifts is important because we consistently face challenges. The stirring is essential, and it comes in three ways: through teaching, through prayer, and through impartation. Stirring the prophetic gifts in large weekend services is not always advisable or most beneficial to the congregation because of the nature of those services. A good place to stir the gifts is in prayer meetings.

CHAPTER 15

Principles of Prophetic Protocol

ANY CHURCH THAT wants to build on an apostolic-prophetic foundation and to experience full benefits and blessings of a healthy prophetic ministry needs to ensure that the prophetic ministry functions with excellence and integrity in the church. Basic protocol is necessary to develop this kind of ministry.

Prophetic protocol is not intended to stifle the gift of prophecy, to control people, or to "quench the Spirit." Its purpose is to facilitate the sharing of accurate prophetic words in an atmosphere of reverence toward God, appreciation of His gifts, and sensitivity to those who prophesy and to those who receive and observe prophetic ministry.

Pastors are responsible to protect the prophetic ministry in their churches and to protect their congregations. They need to fan the flame of the prophetic, but they also need to judge and deal with prophetic words. In the event that a false or inaccurate word is released, great damage can be done quickly. Sometimes, the affects of the damage remain even after a word has been dealt with. The best way to keep this from happening is to establish protocol that protects without controlling.

A Point of Clarification

First Corinthians 14:32 sometimes causes confusion: "The spirits of the prophets are subject to the control of the prophets." Some interpret this verse to mean that the Spirit of God is subject to the Prophet; this is incorrect. The Spirit of God is never subject to us; we are always subject to the Holy Spirit. We do not control the Holy Spirit, and we have no authority or ability to tell Him what to do.

This verse refers to the fact that we have the ability to control the way we express the prophetic spirit. We are able to control the prophetic gift expressed through us. Often, people make the excuse, "God made me say that," or, "I couldn't help myself. That word came out of my mouth before I knew it!" to justify their prophetic words, their style of prophesying, or the types of words they release.

We must realize and always remember that the gift of prophecy is for edification, exhortation, and comfort or encouragement. God's heart in prophecy is to strengthen and encourage the Church. We have the ability to control when and how we release prophetic words. The most important consideration as we prophesy is to do so from a heart of love and to fulfill one of the three key purposes of prophecy (edification, exhortation, and comfort), but we also need to be mindful of our tone of voice, body language, and facial expressions, and to be careful not to speak too long.

The Importance of Protocol

First Corinthians 14:29-31 is clear about prophetic protocol, saying that one person should speak first, then another. This tells us that those who prophesy do have the ability to

discipline themselves. Other-
wise, if there is no control in
a church service or meeting,
chaos will reign. To avoid chaos and confusion, every church
that desires a vital, healthy pro-

> *We must realize and always remember that the gift of prophecy is for edification, exhortation, and comfort.*

phetic ministry must develop and enforce basic guidelines.

As you consider establishing prophetic protocol in your church, consider the following questions:

- Does prophetic ministry take place primarily through individuals or primarily through a presbytery?
- In what settings do prophetic gifts operate—corporate services, prayer meetings, staff meetings, cell groups, etc? Each of these environments will need to be aware of the protocol of the house.
- To whom should prophetic words be submitted?
- How are Prophets, prophetic intercessors, and those with prophetic giftings identified, trained, and released to minister?
- How will you communicate the protocol so everyone will be aware of it?
- How will violations of protocol be addressed?

These questions will hopefully raise additional questions that are specific to your church or ministry and help you develop prophetic protocol appropriate to your organization. After the protocol is set, be sure to communicate it clearly and help people come into alignment with it. If they refuse, loving discipline is in order. Communicate also that no one is exempt from following protocol and that Pastors and leaders are expected to follow it, just as congregations are.

Hosting a Prophet

Once you have worked to establish appropriate prophetic protocol in your church or ministry, it should be enforced consistently and should apply to all who prophesy, including guest ministers. People who come into your church, as your guests, to function prophetically should be informed of and abide by your protocol.

Never allow Prophets to stand up and prophesy the direction of the church. If a Prophet begins to prophesy regarding the direction of the church, confusion may result. Such prophecies should be given to leaders privately and not released publicly unless and until the Pastor deems the release of the word appropriate. The same applies to words of correction; they should be given privately, not publicly.

Also, if you are a leader, do not allow a Prophet to prophesy over you, your family, or your staff publicly without informing you first. If he or she prophesies over you, the congregation will perceive that you have submitted to the Prophet, and have thereby given over your authority to him or her. To avoid this, walk the Prophet through your protocol prior to the service so the word can be judged and affirmed before release.

> *People who come into your church, as your guests, to function prophetically should be informed of and abide by your protocol.*

Six Principles of Prophetic Protocol

1. Always desire and seek to edify, encourage, and comfort. The only proper motivation for prophecy is love. When you prophesy, let your heart be one of desiring to build up and encourage people. When you pray prophetically, pray as though the person for whom you are praying is the most important person in your life and this is your only opportunity to pray for him or her. When you have this attitude, the person will be greatly blessed and encouraged.

2. If you receive a word of direction or correction, or if you have a vision, submit it to the Pastor and realize you have fulfilled your responsibility. Don't push your Pastor to do something with the word or speak against the Pastor if he or she does not affirm or release your word. Unless your Pastor asks you to pray further, then your responsibility ceases with submitting the word to him or her. If a Pastor says "no" to the word, and it comes to pass, don't tell your Pastor "I told you so." If your pastor chooses to affirm the word and releases it from the pulpit, don't nudge people around you and say the word came from you. Your responsibility is to deliver the word. That's all. But please, in addition, pray for your Pastor to have wisdom to judge and discern the word.

3. Offer prophetic words with kindness; do not "force" them on people. Never insist or use prophetic words to "corner" people. When you have a word, offer it to your leaders and give them an opportunity to judge the word and to affirm it without releasing it, affirm and release it, or deny it. Do not try to "enforce" the word or insist that a leader accept a word. The reasons for this are that we can all make mistakes and "miss it," and that even if we are accurate, if a person is not ready to receive a word, then it will not be effective. Never use a prophetic word to manipulate anyone, and do not hold a Pastor "hostage" to a prophetic word.

4. Use words such as, "I sense an impression" or "I feel the Lord is saying to you" instead of "Thus saith the Lord." We should not presume to think we are 100 percent accurate every time we prophesy. We can grow to the level where we can say, "Thus saith the Lord," but it's good to start with, "I sense" or, "I feel." If the prophetic words we give are accurate, they will be just as powerful preceded by, "I sense" as by "Thus saith the Lord." If a word is not from God, no matter how loud we declare or how often we say, "Thus saith the Lord," it will still be inaccurate.

5. Always remain teachable and accountable. None of us has "arrived." We all have things we need to learn and ways in which we need to mature. As we develop in our prophetic giftings, we should constantly desire to learn and grow. We also need to make sure we are accountable to mature, trustworthy people—in life, in ministry, and for the prophetic words we release. Accountability in life and ministry is so important because a strong impartation is released through prophetic prayer and words, so we want to make sure we have "clean hands and a pure heart" (see Psalm 51). We must stay pure before the Lord so that in ministry and impartation, nothing will corrupt that. In addition, every prophetic word we give should be recorded and judged. Be diligent to provide recording equipment, but if a prophecy cannot be recorded in its verbal form, have someone record it in writing as it is being released.

6. Avoid religiosity and prophetic "flakiness." The prophetic ministry is a gift from God designed to be expressed though human beings. When prophesying, people need to be themselves, not try to lower or raise their voices, speak in King James English, be dramatic, dress in clothes they do not typically wear, or shake and tremble, or draw attention to themselves in any way. All such unnatural expressions need to be avoided. God has created all of us in His image, and He does not want us to try to speak, look or act like someone else when we minister.

Section IV:

A Victorious Church

CHAPTER 16

A Firm Foundation for the Church

IN THIS BOOK, I have emphasized the importance of the full restoration of the ministry of Apostles in the contemporary Church. I have also endeavored to make the clear and strong point that the ministry of Prophets must be fully restored in our day. Throughout Scripture, we see that Prophets heard God's voice and declared His word. The Old and New Testament Prophets differ in their roles, yet the fact remains that God has always spoken through His Prophets. This is still true today. I want to sound the trumpet and declare: the Church is in great need of Prophets who function in the full authority of their five-fold office.

According to Ephesians 2:20, Apostles and Prophets lay foundations in the Church. This verse, along with verse 19, teaches us that we are "no longer foreigners and aliens, but fellow citizens with God's people and members of God's household, *built on the foundation of the apostles and prophets . . .*" (emphasis mine). The Church certainly needs a firm

The Church certainly needs a firm foundation today, a solid and unshakable base on which to build and become a light for the world in dark days....

foundation today, a solid and unshakable base on which to build and become a light for the world in dark days, a place of victory in the midst of oppression, and a life-giving institution that has strength to stand against the winds of change that blow so fiercely in the world's societies. This is why the modern-day ministries of Apostles and Prophets are so important; this is why they must work closely together.

We are aware that the five-fold ministries are all important. In fact, they are vital to God's plan for the Church. We are also aware that three of these offices (Evangelist, Pastor, and Teacher) have been working well together for a long time. Those who function in these gifts know how to work together and relate to one another. Congregations know how to relate to those who function in these offices. We know what Evangelists, Pastors, and Teachers do; and we know what to expect from their respective anointings.

It is good that we have recently seen, and are now seeing, more and more Apostles and Prophets properly recognized in the Church than we have seen in the past. Thankfully, the Church is beginning to understand the importance of recognizing these offices. At the same time, we must also face the reality that, in many parts of the world, the ministries of both Apostles and Prophets are still developing and maturing. Much more teaching is needed to help us better understand of the role, character, responsibility, and function of each of these offices/gifts. One of the contributing reasons for this seems to be the fact that we see few functioning relationships between Apostles and Prophets, just as we see few working relationships between Apostles and Pastors. Regrettably, we simply do not have many role models who are showing us how these offices are to relate and work together in ministry. Even though we do not see as many examples as we might like, the importance of these offices working together is as high as ever.

Apostles and Prophets Together

For the Church to fulfill God's purpose and destiny, we must see not only the recognition of Apostles and Prophets, but these two offices "linking" together for increased effectiveness. The Apostle and Prophet represent God's highest governmental offices. They must connect and work together in order to wage war against satan's governmental hierarchy. You see, it takes a kingdom to replace a kingdom; it takes a government to replace a government. Apostles and Prophets are the appointed ones for this "governmental" realm. They represent the governmental authority of God's Kingdom on earth.

These two offices, Apostle and Prophet, must stand together against satan's kingdom, which is a governmental kingdom. They are to pull down satan's governmental kingdom and authority. When Apostles and Prophets stand together, they release a combined power that can change the world!

However, in the world today, many Apostles do not have a working relationship with a Prophet. In fact, I dare say that many Apostles are functioning without a working covenant relationship with a Prophet. Some Apostles have relationships with one or more intercessors, but an intercessor is not a Prophet. A Prophet is an Apostle's peer in five-

To come to maturity, the Church today desperately needs mutually respectful, releasing, honoring, working, covenantal relationships between Apostles and Prophets.

fold ministry. This is a critical point.

To come to maturity, the Church today desperately needs mutually respectful, releasing, honoring, working, covenantal relationships between Apostles and Prophets. This must begin in the local church.

Gifts in the Church

Let me remind you of a key passage of Scripture regarding the five-fold ministry: "It was he [Jesus] who gave some to be apostles, some to be prophets, some to be evangelists, and some to be pastors and teachers to prepare God's people for works of service, so that the body of Christ may be built up. . ." (Ephesians 4:11, 12). Clearly, Ephesians 4:11 teaches us that Jesus Himself personally gave the five ministry gifts or offices we refer to as "the five-fold ministry" and that these gifts were to work together. Where are these gifts to operate? In the body of Christ, according to Ephesians 4:12, and this must begin in the local church.

Therefore, we should be able to nurture, develop, and model the working relationship of both the Apostle and the Prophet, first, in the local church. In fact, all of the gifts should be discovered and developed within the local church. Then, from the local church, these gifts are to be released into the broader body of Christ, the Church universal.

One of the challenges that arises as gifts develop and mature in local churches, especially in regard to Prophets, is that people who think they are Prophets often leave the local church and establish prophetic ministries that are independent of the local church.

When this happens, loss occurs in at least two ways. The first loss is that the prophetic ministry is lost in the local church. Its purpose, which is to serve as an ongoing equipping voice, is no longer realized in the local church. Thus, the true equipping of a new generation of Prophets is absent from the place where it should be happening. The more seasoned Prophets are out building their own ministries instead of raising up new Prophets and prophetic voices in and through the local churches. Some of these people would say that we need to allow emerging prophetic people be to trained at seminars and conferences, but such events can never provide a "safe" environment, week after week, where people who have a prophetic gift can be nurtured, corrected, trained, and encouraged to hear more accurately.

The second loss that occurs in most cases when Prophets leave their local churches is that the Prophets lose the spiritual covering their Pastors provide because they choose to walk out from under it. We must remember that all believers need to be connected with a local church and have pastoral covering, whether we walk in a five-fold ministry office or not.

Related to this, Peter Wagner states that even John Wimber, founder of the Vineyard Churches Association, realized that early in the birthing of the prophetic, he was intimidated by the gifting of the Prophets. He did not know how to "handle" them. This happened early in the restoration process of the Prophets, and he did not know how to relate to them—either to "Pastor" them or maybe, as Peter Wagner suggests, to "Apostle" them (*Apostles and Prophets,* p. 137).

> *We must remember that all believers need to be connected with a local church and have pastoral covering, whether we walk in a five-fold ministry office or not.*

Many pastors today are experiencing the same intimidation, but we must break through intimidation. The five-fold offices *must* learn to work together in mutual respect and submission. The Church's destiny depends on it!

Though I understand how important working relationships between Pastors and Prophets are, I am not going to focus on that in this book. For more on the subject, I highly recommend Peter Wagner's book, *Pastors and Prophets.* Here, I want to focus on an equally-important topic, but one that less has been written about: the relationship between Apostles and Prophets—how they relate to one another in ministry and work together for the building of God's glorious Church.

In the following chapter, I want to focus on the relationship between Apostles and Prophets, and to address the ways these two offices or gifts need to work together to build God's Kingdom. The points and observations I will make about Apostles and Prophets working together are equally relevant to local church settings and to traveling ministries. In fact, anywhere Apostles and Prophets work together, these principles apply.

CHAPTER 17

Effective Teamwork

As I MENTIONED IN the previous chapter, little has been written and made available to the Church at-large on the subject of how Apostles and Prophets are to develop effective working relationships for the building of God's Kingdom. Yet, we know from Ephesians 2:20 that these two offices work together to lay foundations in the Church, so we must begin to understand the practical and spiritual dynamics of effective teamwork between them.

As I have served as an Apostle over the years, I have learned to work with Prophets and been privileged to minister with some exceptional men and women who are called and anointed for the office of the Prophet. I have distilled these lessons into sixteen principles that are necessary for Apostles and Prophets to be fruitful for the Kingdom together.

1. They must share the same vision. Sharing the same vision is essential to the effective teamwork of Apostles and Prophets. In other words, there must be unity of heart between them and they must have a common purpose. This is biblical, based on Amos 3:3: "Can two walk together unless they are agreed?" (NKJV). The agreed-upon vision that Apostles and Prophets need to share must be Kingdom minded. They may do different things in ministry, but neither is trying to build or promote himself or herself, but they are always focused on building others.

2. They must both be "Kingdom minded." As mentioned, Apostles and Prophets should never try to build their own "kingdom." They need to see the body of Christ across denominational lines and across church lines. They must see the whole body of Christ, the entire Kingdom of God, and they must desire to build up everyone in it, not just a few favorites.

3. They must respect and rely on each other. They must have a basic trust in one another and learn to rely on each other. Let's say that one of my Prophets comes and gives me a "word." I can't think, *Well, I wonder why he is saying that. What's he up to? Is there a motive behind what he is telling me?*

There are times when I instruct the Prophets and intercessors in our church: "You go into the prayer room, hear from God, and tell me what He is saying." Now, most of the time, I will have heard something from Him already, but I want to know if they are hearing the same. So, I give them an assignment. I don't tell them what God is saying to me. They pray, and hear from God, and they tell me. That way we can compare what we are hearing to see if we are on track.

This is a way of respecting the Prophets and intercessors; and it's a protection for me. They could hear a warning, or a situation to be on the look-out for in the coming days. As an Apostle, I must be open to receive prophetic words from my Prophets and intercessors. Likewise, they must be open to receive a word from me as well.

4. Apostles and Prophets do not compete. If Apostles and Prophets are going to share Kingdom vision and work together effectively, they must be in harmony. Where there is harmony, there is no competition. For example, if I am ministering with a Prophet, it would be wrong for me to teach for an hour-and-a-half and leave the Prophet only 20 minutes. It would be equally wrong for a Prophet to treat an Apostle that way. Competition for the platform, the microphone, recognition, or a "place" is not of the Kingdom; it comes from a destructive spirit.

5. Prophets hear from God. Amos 3:7 tells us: "Surely the Lord God does nothing unless He reveals His secrets to His servants, the prophets." Thus, the primary responsibility of a Prophet is to hear what God is saying. Of course, everyone can hear from God, but the Prophet has been "graced" by God to especially hear from God at a different level than most others.

6. Prophets submit to Apostles. This principle of spiritual submission is part of God's divine order. Again, 1 Corinthians 12:28 clearly states: "And in the church God has appointed first of all apostles, second prophets, third teachers, then workers of miracles, also those having gifts of healing, those able to help others, those with gifts of administration, and those speaking in different kinds of tongues."

We can see from this verse God's divine order of spiritual authority in the Church. Therefore, Prophets should hear from God, but should submit all "major" impacting (directional) prophetic words to the Apostle for him or her to judge before that word is released.

In reality, this matter of submission is the point where many Prophets struggle. Unwillingness to submit is also the reason many Prophets decide to become Apostles.

However, Scripture clearly tells us in Ephesians 5:21 that we are to "Submit to one another out of reverence for Christ." This verse calls us to a mutual submission. We are all called to be in submission to one another in the fear of God. That's spiritual submission—in the home or in the Church. It is also the guiding principle between Apostles and Prophets. It is not a matter of competition, but of spiritual submission.

7. Apostles and Prophets are peers. Here is where balance and respect are lived out. While Prophets receive the word from God and submit it to the Apostle, they are still peers. Apostles must nurture, encourage, and acknowledge the gift in the Prophet, which is equally important as the gift in the Apostle. One gift is not "better" than another; the two simply function differently.

Because of respect, the Apostle honors the Prophet as a peer, as an equal, as a fellow minister, as someone who has a gift from God. Then as they are linked together, they will both be stronger and more effective. The two function as peers, as equals in a relationship. One does not try to control or dictate the other, but they have a working relationship, a functioning relationship, a relationship where they each "prefer" the other.

If we honor all of the gifts, then no one feels like a "second-class citizen," because we realize that all of the gifts are of equal importance and those who operate in the gifts are peers, even though they have different functions in the body of Christ.

8. The Apostle judges, evaluates, strategizes, and executes the word. Apostles are to judge heresy and to bring discipline and correction when needed. Like the Apostle Paul, they will judge problems in the church, and judge individuals for misconduct and moral sins. Apostles are to also "judge" major impacting prophetic words and they carry the responsibility of hearing from God concerning strategies needed to facilitate, prepare, and execute God's prophetic word so it can be fulfilled.

9. Apostles and Prophets are to complement one another. Iron sharpens iron. That doesn't mean Apostles and Prophets do not correct each other, or that we always agree. It's important that each one help the other work better and with greater manifestation of God's Kingdom in every way. As Apostles and Prophets work together in a complementary way, we should begin to experience less confusion and more strategic results in spiritual warfare and transformation.

10. Apostles and Prophets sense that their callings and ministries are linked together. Somewhere in the sense of their destiny in God, Apostles and Prophets know they are linked together for Kingdom purposes. They can say to each other, "Some way, my gift will help your ministry grow and become more impacting and vice versa. We can still function in our own separate meetings or we can work together in the same meetings. However, because we are in a working relationship with one another, we'll be stronger and accomplish more."

11. Apostles and Prophets are team players. Apostles and Prophets not only work as players on a team, they are deeply committed to the philosophy of team ministry.

Let me explain. For many years, churches had only one Pastor. Then, we began to move toward a "multiple staff" model, in which we had more than one Pastor—a children's Pastor, a youth Pastor, and an associate Pastor, for example. Sometimes people think that multiple staff equals team ministry. It does not. An organization can have multiple staff without having a team. Usually with a multiple staff situation, each person focuses almost exclusively on his or her personal area of responsibility. In other words, each area becomes a person's own individual "kingdom."

Team ministry differs from a multiple staff approach in that each team member has areas of responsibility, but also sees the church as a whole. They will realize that the vision of the church is holistic. All of them will be very aware that what they do in their areas of oversight will impact the other team members, the corporate vision of the church, and the church as a whole. The team should be working and contributing together for overall impact, not individual impact. In other words, all planning is done corporately together in planning sessions. During that time of planning, all ministry plans are subjected to scrutiny to assure that each ministry is providing a vital link toward the overall church vision becoming a reality during a quarter, during a year, or over a five-year period.

The way I like to think of the five-fold ministry is to compare them to a rugby team. Although I do not know the rules of rugby, I have seen teams passing the ball forward, backward, sideways, through their legs, and over their heads. It's incredible to watch how they move that ball! The one outstanding thing is this: the team has a leader (captain), but they all work together to get to the goal, regardless of who carries the ball across. They win as a team, not as individuals. To me, that is the best picture of the teamwork of the Apostle, Prophet, Evangelist, Pastor, and Teacher working and flowing together for Kingdom purposes.

12. Apostles and Prophets must communicate and pray with each other on a regular basis. Apostles and Prophets must contact each other often, and pray with each other. They should have an agreed-upon timetable whereby they pray together on a regular basis. "Regular" could be every day, once a week, twice a week, or once a month. They simply need to agree upon how often they will do it and when. Then both of them work with their respective schedules to make it happen.

How can we develop or maintain relationships with other people if we never communicate? Although time is precious for all of us yet, getting together with people in person is critically important, but can often be difficult because of the pressure of time. Here is where the blessing of technology comes in. We can provide much encouragement, prayer, and mentoring by e-mail, text messages (SMS), Skype, or phone calls. Thank God for the technology that helps us improve in this area!

13. Apostles and Prophets must cultivate accountable covenant relationships. One of the crucial values of the restoration of Apostles and Prophets today is accountability. We must have accountable, covenant relationships within the body of Christ. This requires us to walk in humility. We must humble ourselves and recognize that we are not "the only one." We need others in the body and we need account-able, "peer-level" relationships with others.

We see at least two models of this in the Bible. Paul and Silas had an ongoing relationship; they covenanted together, and they demonstrate to us a long-term, working, covenant relationship. Paul and Agabus also provide an example of an accountable relationship, but they were linked or tied to-gether for a shorter period of time in ministry.

In my life, I have several such relationships. For example, Dominic Yeo is one of my Prophets and has been for several years. He began as our "church" Prophet in Trinity Christian Centre in Singapore, and now he has been recognized as a national Prophet in Singapore. He serves as an international representative on the Apostolic Council of Prophetic Elders (ACPE) in the USA. Another of my Prophets, Ong Sek Leang, who is a Senior Pastor from Kuala Lumpur (KL), Malaysia also serves on this council.

Ong Sek Leong also speaks into my life and into our church. Sometimes he will call me or Pastor Dominic Yeo from KL. Sometimes he will even fly from KL to Singapore for the sole purpose of delivering a "word" he has received from the Lord because he feels the word is that important. When he visits us in person with a word from God, he deliv-ers the word to me. He does not always preach in the pulpit when he comes. The congregation never knows he was here, and neither do we give him "an offering" because he came with a word. He is not seeking a platform, nor is he trying to gain influence into our church. He is simply carrying out his responsibility as a Prophet who is in relationship with me and with our church.

Pastor Gerald Tan, who is currently on our Leadership Team of the church and serves as one of our two District

Overseers in Trinity Christian Centre (TCC), is also our "warring Prophet." He travels with me to other nations, helping train leaders in the apostolic and prophetic. In fact, both Pastors Gerald and Ong Sek Leang are part of our prophetic training team in many nations.

Both in Malaysia and Singapore, in our respective local churches, we have a School of the Prophets. Also, because we train and nurture the five-fold ministry gifts, we have many Prophets and a number of emerging Apostles in our churches.

14. Pride will kill relationships. Humility is a key characteristic of an Apostle. Humility is the opposite of pride, and it will devastate the relationships that need to exist between Apostles and Prophets, and between Apostles and others. However, it is important to remember that no one is born humble. Humility is a decision we make. Matthew 23:12 says: "whoever exalts himself will be humbled, and whoever humbles himself will be exalted." Humility, along with character, is considered one of the most important signs of a true Apostle. If you believe you are an Apostle, can you humble yourself to serve others? Can you humble yourself to feel someone else's pain? Can you build up others and not just yourself? An Apostle must function in humility and as a servant.

It is important to remember that pride is an area that all ministers, including those in five-fold offices, will always need to battle. Pride which led to rebellion first manifested itself in the Garden of Eden. It is still a tool the devil will use to destroy ministries.

You see, every time God answers your prayer, every time God does a miracle that you are a part of—look out, pride can begin to develop in your spirit. The accolades of people about how "good you are," "how much you blessed them," "how powerful your ministry is"—these are wonderful to hear, but they can also become stumbling blocks if we do not handle the issue of pride in our hearts.

15. Apostles and Prophets flow in greater authority when they flow together than when they operate independently. As mentioned earlier, Apostles and Prophets are powerful when their anointings are combined together in spiritual warfare. Therefore, if in any way their authority is undermined, we begin to experience problems in local churches and in the body of Christ.

In Colombia, South America, we have seen the power of restoring and recognizing their Apostles and Prophets in the nation. I recall the first time we gathered some of the Apostles and Prophets in that nation to come together to agree on what was happening spiritually in their nation.

At the close of the meeting, I told them we were going to pray—but that they could only pray if they partnered together as Apostle and Prophet. Thus they had to look out among the group, identify one another's gift/anointing. If you were an Apostle, you had to find a Prophet and vice versa. Only then could the two standing together begin to pray for the nation of Colombia. The Apostle and Prophet as God's highest governmental authority began to pray and make declarations into the heavens.

Shortly thereafter, I began to read in the newspaper about the rescues of people who had been kidnapped. This had not happened before. Now it was happening. Many of us are firmly convinced that their Apostles and Prophets praying together, in the authority of their offices, turned the tide of this problem in Colombia.

16. Apostles serving as an "apostolic covering" to others. When we are talking about an Apostle, you must understand that you don't "link up" with or come under apostolic covering today and then break off the relationship tomorrow. When you establish a "covenant relationship" with an Apostle, it's like a marriage; you go through the good and bad times, the ups and downs together. You do not casually break covenant. However, if for some reason you have "bonded" and entered into a covenant relationship that is not good, the question that often arises is, "Can I get out of a bad covenant relationship?" The answer is yes, it is possible to "break" that covenant. But you must do it properly and in a spirit of honor.

If an Apostle provides covering for you, that person should be someone who will love and honor you. In the same way, you must submit to that person's discipline if you are out of order. Now, this is the very thing that frightens some people.

This is why the Apostle who provides you with "covering" must be someone with whom you have a trusting relationship and you are confident they are mentoring and speaking into your life with no hidden agenda.

Apostles should not be there to "lord" over you but to protect you, to help you get what you need for your ministry to have credibility, and to take you to the next level. An Apostle is there to bring order and blessing into your ministry.

Church, hear me: the gifts and ministries of Apostles and Prophets—and those of the intercessors—*must* be re-established in the Church. We need people trained to pray, but more than "petition" prayers. Believers must be trained as prophetic intercessors.

I firmly believe that our lack of strong, trained intercessors contributes to our lack of strong, functioning Prophets. I have observed over the years that it is from our "pool" of strong prophetic intercessors that we will begin to discover our emerging Prophets. It is all of these gifts, especially now including the Apostle and Prophet, working together that will build a people, a Church, with the strength to stand in our day.

Moment of Decision

THE CHURCH TODAY is at a crossroads. Are we content to hold mere religious gatherings without power? Or do we want to become a world-impacting expression of the Kingdom of God? In order to turn the tide in how we do "church," we need a radical makeover. That involves making a decision to change the way we do things and being conformed to God's way.

The starting point is to read and heed God's Word. Then our radical makeover happens as we apply its truth to a model that works for transforming the Church into a life-changing manifestation of God's authority.

Let's begin by looking at the Apostle Paul's letter to the church in Rome. In Romans 12:2 he instructed them not to be conformed to the world's way of doing things: "Do not conform any longer to the pattern of this world…"

For too many years we have misunderstood the real meaning of this verse. We have eloquently expounded that scripture, saying it is about what clothes women should avoid wearing, why we should *not* watch TV or go to movies, plus a long list of other "sins" that we associate with the "world."

If we think about it, TV, movies, and many of the things we connect with Romans 12:2 were not problems in ancient Rome because the technology was not there. Most of these items had not yet been invented! It is clear to me that Paul was addressing deeper issues. Allow me to suggest some of the things Paul was challenging believers *not* to be conformed to.

First of all, I believe that Paul was encouraging the people not to be conformed any longer to the religious system or the worship system that was blinding them to God's revelation. He was saying do not be conformed to the present value system of this world. Do not do business in the same manner, with the same values as this present world system is doing business. When you do business their way, you can clearly see that it leads to corruption and greed.

The believers in Rome surely understood what Paul was saying and knew it was necessary for changes to take place. But how? The "world's" system was so entrenched, so established, so much the norm for every area of life, business and religion. Fortunately, Paul gave them a plan. In Romans 12:2, he followed through by explaining what action they should take: "...but be transformed by the renewing of your mind. Then you will be able to test and approve what God's will is—his good, pleasing and perfect will."

Paul taught them that transformation—change that shifts things from one paradigm to another—all begins in our individual mind. The first step to real transformation is realizing that we need renewed minds that can think differently. We need our minds to be impacted by God's Word and the Holy Spirit until we have the very mind of Christ. We need to embrace God's Kingdom values and apply them in every area of life—in our work, business, government, and church.

Friends, there are clear guidelines in the Word of God that give us principles we can adopt and incorporate into our churches that will enable us to function as the Church Jesus desired to build. Stick with me as I introduce you to a model of small groups that apply what I have been talking about.

A Model for Transformation

The Carecell model was developed in Trinity Christian Centre, a vibrant, thriving church in Singapore. I believe that Trinity is one of the most effective, most cutting-edge apostolic-prophetic churches in the world today and serves as a powerful model for others.

One of the ministry arms of Trinity Christian Centre is the Global Leadership Network (GLN)—a network of believers committed to fulfilling the Great Commission in our generation worldwide. The mission of the Global Leadership Network is to empower churches to transform the harvest *field* into a harvest *force* by training, consulting, mentoring, and equipping with relevant resources (available in many languages) for nurturing, training and leadership development.

Through GLN and the Pastors of Trinity Christian Centre, the Carecell model has laid an apostolic foundation in many churches. This has enabled them to reach their communities for Christ, to help believers discover their spiritual gifts (especially the five fold offices), and to equip believers to become discipled leaders (and not managers) in the Kingdom.

Leadership development is a key outcome of Carecells. Only when the Church develops real Kingdom leaders will we reproduce believers who will have the strength to stand in the shifting time in which we live. I will now write to you specifically about the model that has proven effective when God transforms our old ways of thinking into new ways that change us and impact our world.

Background and Overview of the
GLN Cell Church Model

For almost 30 years, I served as senior Pastor in Trinity Christian Centre in Singapore. In 2004, after a strategic leadership transition process that spanned a number of years, Rev. Dominic Yeo became senior Pastor, and I moved into the position of resident Apostle. We built the church, the flagship church of Global Leadership Network, to its present strength using the GLN Cell Church Model. The church continues to grow in size and in maturity using this approach to ministry.

Literally thousands of churches have been established throughout the world using the GLN Cell Church Model. This model is easily transferable and can be implemented in all kinds of believing churches. The "kinks" have been worked out so that the model functions at optimum efficiency to produce maximum benefit. Also, Trinity members are available to assist leaders in any church to implement this model.

The GLN Cell Church Model is a biblical model that releases the five-fold ministries for the purpose of equipping God's people to fulfill the ministry of reconciliation. The result is a church that is aligned with God's divine order as expressed in Ephesians 4:11-16:

It was he who gave some to be apostles, some to be prophets, some to be evangelists, and some to be pastors and teachers, to prepare God's people for works of service, so that the body of Christ may be built up until we all reach unity in the faith and in the knowledge of the Son of God and become mature, attaining to the whole measure of the fullness of Christ. Then we will no longer be infants, tossed back and forth by the waves, and blown here and there by every wind of teaching and by the cunning and craftiness of men in their deceitful scheming. Instead, speaking the truth in love, we will in all things grow up into him who is the Head, that is, Christ. From him the whole body, joined and held together by every supporting ligament, grows and builds itself up in love, as each part does its work.

A church built on the GLN Cell Church Model becomes a church in which 1 Peter 2:9 becomes a reality: "But you are *a chosen people, a royal priesthood, a holy nation,* a people belonging to God, that you may declare the praises of him who called you out of darkness into his wonderful light" (emphasis mine). To accomplish this goal, the GLN Model cultivates churches in which all believers live with a sense of destiny, fulfilling God's call and purpose for their lives wherever they may be—in their families, in their workplaces, or at school. It develops churches in which believers are released to serve God and people by actively praying for, winning, and nurturing others to bring them back to God. In addition it produces churches in which everyone is set free to grow in godly character and transformed to be like Christ.

In the GLN Cell Church Model, equipping the saints is accomplished through two tracks: the Carecell Track and the Training Track. Let me first explain the Carecell Track.

The Carecell Track

The foundation of the GLN Cell Church Model is the carecell—a spiritual family in which people gather to experience God through relationships with one another. In carecells, people feel the pulse and life of the church, and they experience the warmth of genuine fellowship and the excitement of being disciples of Christ. Carecells provide atmospheres in which people can receive support and encouragement, learn practical principles and truths to overcome challenges in life, and grow and discover God's purposes.

There are four primary strengths of the GLN Cell Church Model:

- *A culture of evangelism.* Every believer in the carecell is trained and released in evangelism. This results in multiplication of the open carecells and in church growth.
- *A culture of nurture.* People are properly nurtured until they develop the maturity to become spiritual parents. This results in spiritual growth and fruitfulness.
- *A culture of leadership development.* New leaders are constantly being spotted and groomed, and leaders are continually discipled in knowledge, character, and skills. This results in an expanding leadership base that facilitates expanding vision.
- *A culture of pastoral care.* Every person in a carecell receives quality pastoral care.

The Carecell Track provides relational discipleship in the context of community through "open carecells" and "leadership carecells." Open carecells meet weekly, and their purpose is to provide opportunities for evangelism and discipleship. The goal of open carecells is multiplication for the purpose of community transformation.

Leadership carecells meet once every two weeks for the purpose of developing and growing leadership. There are three key strengths of leadership carecells:

- *Discipleship:* Being mentored and having someone to be accountable to.
- *Leadership development:* Developing spiritual gifts through serving.
- *Community life:* Receiving peer support and encouragement from other leaders.

The Training Track

The Training Track provides training in Bible skills, life skills, and ministry skills. The Training Track's purpose is to impart Kingdom vision, values, and skills, and its goal is leadership development. It accomplishes this through pulpit ministry, courses and seminars such as spiritual parenting, carecell leaders' training, Leadership Community Empowerment (training and equipping for leaders), and the Divine Exchange and Wholeness ministry that deals with inner healing and deliverance.

Training in pulpit ministry takes place weekly; courses and seminars take place when necessary, and Leadership Community Empowerment takes place monthly or once every two or three months.

The Result of Using this Model

Together, the Carecell Track and the Training Track provide a strong leadership development path that produces believers who obey the Great Commandments and fulfill the Great Commission. These believers are able to live and function in community according to God's original purpose and are well equipped for the ministry of reconciliation.

To learn more about the GLN Cell Church Model, visit www.gln.com.sg.

Global Leadership Network Resources and Contact Information

GLN resources are now available in 13 languages! GLN Resources are available in the following languages: English, Chinese (Traditional & Simplified Script), Hindi, Indonesian, Japanese, Kannada, Malayalam, Polish, Spanish, Tamil, Telegu, and Thai.

Contact information:

Singapore Office
Global Leadership Network
247 Paya Lebar Road
#03-01 Singapore 409045
Tel: (65) 63047768
Fax: (65) 67430178
Email: admin@gln.com.sg
Website: www.gln.com.sg

USA Office
Global Leadership Network
1042 E. Fort Union #114
Midvale, UT 84047
United States of America

Office: (801) 243-7301
Fax: (801) 406-0194
Email: info@glnusa.com

Colombia Office
Global Leadership Network
(Red Mundial De Liderazgo)
Cra 14 #76-39 of 701
Barrio El Lago
Bogota, Colombia
Telefax: 57 1 256 4401
Email: evm_gln@etb.net.co

Resources

Nurturing Series

New Beginnings: *Laying Key Foundations in Your Life & Your Relationships*

New Choices: *That Unlock the Blessings of Obedience*

New Steps: *To Spiritual Breakthrough & Freedom*

New Calling: *Discover Your Identity, Fulfill Your Destiny*

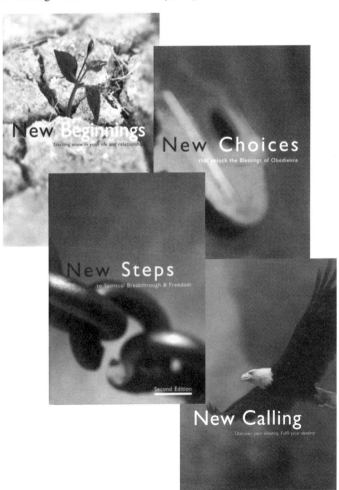

Accompanying Tools

Book of Life: An innovative tool that helps every Christian become an active soul-winner

Time Alone with God bookmark: A bookmark that guides the Christian in his Time Alone with God

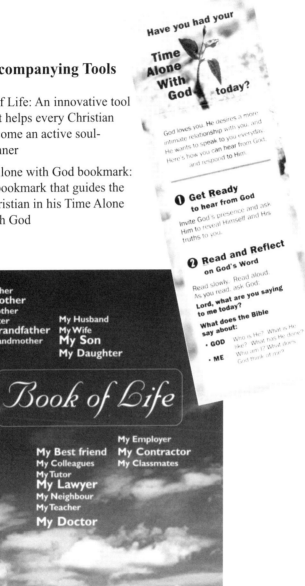

Have you had your **Time Alone With God** today?

God loves you. He desires a more intimate relationship with you, and He wants to speak to you everyday. Here's how you can hear from God, and respond to Him.

❶ Get Ready to hear from God

Invite God's presence and ask Him to reveal Himself and His truths to you.

❷ Read and Reflect on God's Word

Read slowly. Read aloud. As you read, ask God:

Lord, what are you saying to me today?

What does the Bible say about:

• **GOD** — Who is He? What is He like? What has He done?

• **ME** — Who am I? What does God think of me?

My Father
My Mother
My Brother
My Sister   My Husband
My Grandfather My Wife
My Grandmother   **My Son**
                   My Daughter

Book of Life

                    My Employer
My Best friend **My Contractor**
My Colleagues   My Classmates
My Tutor
My Lawyer
My Neighbour
My Teacher

My Doctor

This Book of Life belongs to:

Leadership Development Series

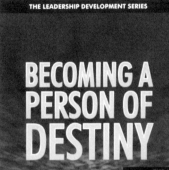

Becoming a Person of Destiny:
Joining Abraham on his journey of discipleship

Becoming a Person of Destiny 2:
Learning to walk by faith with the God of Abraham

Becoming a Person of Destiny 3:
Understanding the heart of the God of Abraham

Children's Resources

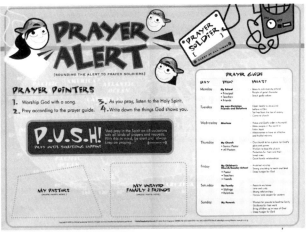

Training Tools

Spiritual Parent Trainers'
  Guide

Seven Steps to Transforming
  Your Church

CareCell Leaders Trainer's
  Guide

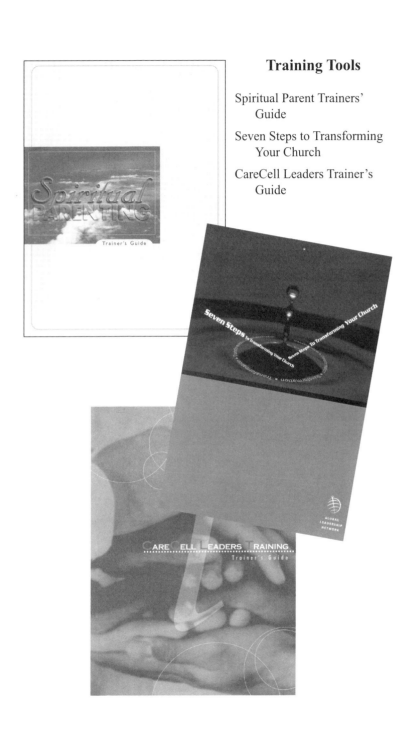